MAKE YOUR OWN SAILS

MAKE YOUR OWN SAILS

BY
R. M. BOWKER
AND
S. A. BUDD

MACMILLAN

First Edition February 1957
Reprinted October 1957, 1959
Second Edition 1960
Reprinted 1962, 1966, 1969
Revised Edition 1975
SBN: 333 01050 7

Published by
MACMILLAN LONDON LTD
London and Basingstoke
and also at Johannesburg Melbourne
New York Dublin and Delhi

Printed in Hong Kong by
Dai Nippon Printing Co (H.K.) Ltd

INTRODUCTION

THIS is a handbook for those who desire to make their own sails. With the aid of it, and with care and mental application, we believe that anyone can make for himself sails the equal of any manufactured commercially. We hope that the book will also be of interest to those who wish to advance their knowledge of sailmaking, the matter being so arranged that technical instructions need only be read if sailmaking is actually in progress.

In our view, it is a great help to anyone who makes sails to be conversant with the theory of sailing, for the real art of sailmaking must lie in translating knowledge of sailing and sails to the sail loft floor. The actual manufacture, though requiring skill and technique, is a mechanical process; the design of the sail, on the other hand, is the part so greatly assisted by sailing experience.

The reader may feel, at first glance, that to make his own sails is too difficult a task without some expert knowledge, especially when it comes to dealing with the design of the floor sail plan, where there is so much room for the exercise of his own judgement. But we would ask him not to be discouraged. It is now a proven fact that an amateur without previous experience can make satisfactory sails from written instructions (instructions, in fact, from which this book has been developed). These give all the information required to make a normal average sail, and the reader should find no difficulty in following them and putting them into practice.

We wish him real and lasting success in his venture, whether it be for his own amusement or for financial reward.   THE AUTHORS

CONTENTS

ILLUSTRATIONS

NOTE

FOR those who are embarking on amateur sailmaking, we suggest the study of existing sails, particularly old ones which may be taken to pieces, while your work is in progress, as this will assist in making our explanations and instructions clear.

Choose, if possible, a sail by a well-known sailmaker, as an inexpertly made sail might be misleading. And if you find the sail differs from the advice we give on methods of construction, please do not blame either, as, though the broad principles of sailmaking are more or less fixed, the styling of the details is to a large extent a matter of judgement and choice.

Some parts of this book originally appeared in several issues of *Yachting Monthly*, and grateful acknowledgement is made to the Editor of that journal for permission to reprint the material here.

Additional note 1975. While the majority of professionally built sails are now made in synthetic cloths, nevertheless we offer the text in the present form, for the basis of sailmaking in synthetic sailcloths is exactly the same as for cotton and flax, but with certain adjustments to allow for the different characteristics of the synthetics. This arrangement enables the reader to make excellent synthetic sails and also workable sails out of anything he pleases or of any fabric which he happens to have, whether or not this has been made as a sailcloth.

CHAPTER I

THE THEORY AND PRACTICE OF
SAILS AND SAILMAKING

IN a sense, a sail operates in the same way as an aeroplane's wing, though the job it does is quite different. The wing, in simple form, as in Fig. 1, is so shaped and positioned that the air flowing over the top is speeded up, and that below is slowed down. It will be seen from the

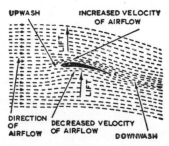

FIG. 1. Section of aeroplane's wing, showing areas of increased and decreased pressure.

Fig. 1 that the air lines above the wing are closer together, and those below further apart, indicating the relative changes in speed. By the venturi effect, the pressure above the wing is reduced, and that below increased.

In order to appreciate how the pressure is affected by the change in speed of the air, it is necessary to see why an ordinary venturi works. A venturi tube has a large opening each end and tapers towards the middle to a small opening through which all the air that enters the tube has to pass. In order to get through, the air naturally must pass through the central hole at a much greater speed than that of the air outside the tube. In so doing, the pressure is reduced on the principle ideally illustrated by a column of soldiers, say six deep, marching along a road in which is set a single file bridge across a river. The bridge represents the small hole in the middle of the venturi tube. While the

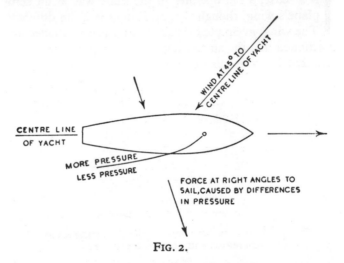

FIG. 2.

column is crossing the bridge, the soldiers actually on the bridge must run at a very high speed if they are not to hold up the rear of the column approaching the bridge and to catch up the front which is marching away. And clearly, these men crossing the bridge will be very much further apart from each other than they were when in the column, and their 'pressure' will be reduced.

The effect of the decrease in pressure above the wing,

and increase below, is to tend to make the wing move upwards, or resist the downward pull of gravity. In the case
of the aeroplane all this force is utilised, but a boat is
actually designed to prevent the force from operating.
Fig. 2 shows that when close-hauled, the sail, though the
same shape as the upper surface of the wing, presents a
very much coarser angle of incidence to the direction of
movement of the air. There is a much more marked difference in pressure between the windward and leeward
sides, causing a great deal more 'lift' and at the same time,
more drag. Fig. 2 shows that as far as possible the 'lift', or
tendency to make leeway, is nullified by the boat's keel,
but the essential point is that the 'lift' operates in a direction slightly forward of the beam, and the leeway having
been stopped there is a residue of force left to drive the
boat in a forward direction, being the only direction between a point at right angles to the beam and dead ahead
that the boat can move.

The comparison between the sail and the aircraft's wing
is an enlightening one, but it should not, we feel, be
carried too far. The main difference would seem to be that
the sail operates at an angle of incidence to the air greatly
in excess of that required by the wing, and that the 'lift'
produced by the sail is forced to drive the sail in a forward
direction, a thing which is never made to happen in the
case of a wing.

* * * * *

Although it is quite possible to make sails successfully
without sailing experience — either from experience, or by
obeying written instructions implicitly — we are sure
that knowledge of sailing will be found to be a great help
in making higher quality sails. And, of course, this know-

ledge should cover all aspects of the matter. From cruising, one learns the importance of long service and reliability; from racing, efficiency; and perhaps from ocean racing both, though in any handicap race, where the vessels are structurally different, travelling at different speeds and reacting differently to varying weather conditions, the finer points of efficiency are inevitably hidden. Dinghy racing and sailing is important also, but not quite so much so, as all the requirements for a dinghy sail are incorporated in those for larger vessels, whereas many details essential for larger sails are not to be found in the small ones.

A sail is never in the normal way made perfectly flat, but is given a certain predetermined flow or fullness, principally by cutting as convex curves the sides of the sail that lie along spars or stays (immediately the curved side is stretched straight, a belly appears in the sail). It is easy to see that the sail should be made as full as practicable for the particular job it has to do, in order to give maximum efficiency (a full parachute naturally would fall more slowly than a flat one). For windward work, there can obviously be very little fullness, if the sail is to set; but for running before the wind, there should be as much fullness as possible, the parachute spinnaker being a very full sail indeed. Thus, in theory, the further off the wind the yacht is heading, the fuller should the sail be; but, of course, it is usually impracticable to carry and change sails for different points of sailing, and the best that can be done is to ensure that the sail in use is the best, on average, for the yacht.

Sailing craft vary in shape and performance a very great deal, from the Metre yacht, long and slender, with high windward performance, to, say, the Dutchman, which has comparatively little windward ability. The latter should obviously have full sails to give maximum speed off the wind, whereas it is of paramount importance for the former to have sails designed for sailing on the wind, the advantage gained here immeasurably outweighing any loss of efficiency down wind.

The shapes of sails are largely controlled by physical limitations. Theoretically, it is of no great importance where the mast is stepped, right forward or aft, or in an intermediate position, and whether all the canvas is in one large sail or divided into several. But in practice, a single masted yacht is almost bound to have the mast stepped a little forward of amidships in order to keep the sails properly set. If the mast is too far forward, staying the mast will be difficult due to narrowness of the hull; if aft, the running stays will not be powerful enough to keep the forestay tight. A 12-Metre was once rigged with the mast well aft of amidships, having a very short boom, and an immense foresail area. We understand that the rig was perfectly satisfactory except for the fatal difficulty that the running stays were totally inadequate.

Again, in theory, loose-footed sails are better, but practical considerations rule that almost every mainsail is fitted to a boom. This is partly because the hull has not usually sufficient length for sheeting a loose-footed mainsail home, and partly because the loss of efficiency in fitting the foot to a boom is small and is far more than compensated by the ease of handling that the boom supplies. Neither of these two difficulties apply to foresails, so that in nearly every case these are loose-footed.

★   ★   ★   ★   ★

Perhaps the most fundamental part of sailmaking is the laying of the cloth, and the appreciation as to why it must

B

be so laid. Along the warp or weft, an average sailcloth will stretch little; but at an angle, the amount of stretch will be very great (try this with a handkerchief, stretching it first along one side, and then across diagonally opposite corners. In the latter case it is not the yarns that are stretching, but the shape of the whole handkerchief that is being altered, the line of stretch increasing, as it were, at the expense of the rest of the handkerchief). Thus there are two ways in which a sail may stretch, stretching in either way or in both at once.

This being so, the cloths in any triangular sail are arranged so that the sides which cut the cloth at an angle are prevented from stretching by rope or wire (cf. the luff and foot of a Bermudian mainsail, and the luff of a foresail), the remaining side or sides merely being reinforced by extra cloth (tabling) (cf. leech of mainsail and foot and leech of foresail).

Having in this way planned the sail so that it will retain its shape in use, it merely remains to finish it in such a way as to ensure that its strength will be sufficient to withstand all possible demands upon it. The methods by which this is achieved have been evolved over the years and have, in fact, changed little in the past century.

The principles of sailmaking, detailed hereafter, are all very obvious to the experienced sailmaker, but if you should be about to embark upon this craft with the aid of this book, we recommend that you proceed as follows: take a brief glance first at Chapter 2 on Sailcloths, to make sure that the sailcloth you have in mind to use is suitable; next skim through Chapter 3 so that you are conversant with its contents. Proceed then to study one of Chapters 4-8, whichever is applicable. During your reading of the sailmaking instructions you will be referred to Chapter 3 for information on how the various sailmaking operations are carried out. And during the manufacture of the sail, it is desirable to study at leisure the last two chapters, for future reference and a fuller knowledge of the subject.

*   *   *   *   *

The sailmaking instructions in each case assume that the dimensions and specification of the sail are known. Before proceeding with the making of a particular sail the measurements of each side, and the tack angle in the case of 4-sided sails, should be decided (the usual tack angle for a mainsail is 87°).

If the boat is being built from a designer's plans, the sail plan showing all the measurements will be included. Where sails are being renewed, the dimensions can be taken from the old sails. If the old sails are not available, and the designer is known, it would be worth applying to him, as probably he would be able to supply a sail plan. In cases where no detailed information is available, and where the amateur sailmaker does not feel he has enough technical knowledge to design his sail plan, it would be best to seek expert advice.

CHAPTER 2

SAILCLOTHS

SAILCLOTHS vary considerably in style, quality and cost, and it is worth considering their respective merits in the light of the jobs they are required to do. For instance, if the yacht is the heavy cruising type which cannot go well to windward in any case, it would not be economical to pay extra for a cloth which keeps its shape better but which is no stronger. Alternatively, for racing where the set of the sail is of paramount importance, it would be unwise to economise on the sailcloth. Again, if the sail is left in the weather permanently the stress should be on lasting quality, and so on.

The cloths in general use comprise the following: Egyptian cotton, American cotton, flax, terylene (or the American equivalent dacron) and nylon. We list the respective merits below, but we would stress that the way in which the cloth is woven is an important factor in its quality. In general the tighter the weave the better the cloth.

Egyptian cotton

It so happens that the best grade cotton comes from Egypt, and it is distinguishable by its slightly creamy colour, which in sails looks very well indeed, though it gradually disappears in use. Until very recently, all the best yacht sails were made from Egyptian cotton woven by sailcloth specialists, though now terylene and dacron seem likely in due course to supersede expensive cotton sailcloth. Best Egyptian cotton sailcloth is extremely tightly

8

and accurately woven, with straight selvedge edges, and usually comes in pieces of 100 yards, 18 in. or 36 in. wide, the heavier weights being mainly woven in 18 in. to avoid having to false-seam the cloth, this being less desirable for large sails. Lesser quality Egyptian cotton sailcloths are also obtainable.

American cotton

American cotton is not generally woven specifically for sailcloth, but rather for general purpose canvas, or duck, except in the case of ADM which is sailcloth woven to Admiralty specification. Good cotton duck, however, is suitable for cruising sails, though it does not keep its shape as well as the Egyptian cotton, its tendency to stretch being greater.

The cloth itself is distinguishable by its much whiter appearance, generally coarser weave, rougher finish and the presence as a rule of dark specks, which are cotton seeds. It also feels softer for the same weight of cloth. It is usually woven in pieces of 100 yards 36 in. wide, but may also be obtained in 72 in. wide. The cost is about half that of the best Egyptian cotton sailcloth.

Flax

Flax was in almost universal use for sails in the old sailing ship days, as it has far greater resistance to rot than has cotton. It is also stronger and is very disinclined to tear. On the other hand, it stretches more and a flax sail will lose its shape more easily than a cotton one. In square riggers this point was of no importance, but in fore-and-aft yachts it should be considered. Flax does, however, have a very real advantage over cotton for cruising in that it is very much more easily handled when wet, cotton tending to become very stiff.

To look at, flax sailcloth is a grey-brown colour and is usually coarsely woven. Mixtures of flax and jute are available, but care should be taken to choose only pure flax (which incidently is merely a coarser version of linen). Normally this would come under the heading of R.N. flax, though no doubt other pure flax cloths can be found.

Pure flax can be distinguished from mixtures and from jute by the weave, which in flax is fairly even, whereas the jute yarns vary in thickness, with lumps here and there, producing a rather rough appearance; by the texture, quite smooth in flax but hairy and coarse in jute; and by the colour, flax being a grey-brown and jute a definite brown, much the same as the average colour of hessian.

Terylene (Dacron)

This new fibre was invented in 1941 by members of the Calico Printers Association, of Manchester, as a by-product of oil refining; and was patented. The patent was sold outright to Du Pont of U.S.A., who called their fibre Dacron; and Imperial Chemical Industries were granted sole rights for the rest of the world, naming their product Terylene. In their turn they licensed numbers of firms in other countries to make the fibre, under different names if they chose — the Japanese, for instance, call it Tetoron.

Terylene's special properties for sailmaking are (a) it is smoother, and therefore more efficient in racing, (b) it is not liable to rot — though it can, under sufficient provocation, be disfigured by mildew, (c) it is much easier to handle when wet. Its limitations are (a) the thread of the seams cannot sink into the cloth, and are thus liable to chafe, especially if too large a needle has been used in the machine, (b) it is more liable to creasing than cotton, (c) it is liable to rot if left for long periods in sunlight. Sails should not be left exposed to sunlight when the boat is not in use.

Terylene sailcloths can vary in quality, from the best in the world, to very bad. A good cloth should be woven as tightly as possible. For instance a good 4 oz. cloth would be woven in 125 denier, with warp counting 110 yarns per inch, and weft 80; or 6½ oz. cloth in 250 denier, with warp 70 and weft 64; then it must be shrunk to the maximum extent possible (this is about 10 per cent along both warp and weft, sometimes more). If the weave is loose, or the shrinkage less, a poor cloth results.

The test of a Terylene cloth is to pull it on the bias. A good cloth will feel stable, as does a sheet of paper; but a poor one will stretch on the cross like elastic or any ordinary woven fabric. Where the weave is seen to be a fairly coarse one, yet the stability is good, a stronger bias pull should be exerted to see if the stability is a temporary one, induced by first-class finishing on a poor loom-state fabric. If so, the yarns will be torn from each other by the strong pull, and the stability considerably reduced. The use of such a fabric can result in good sails suddenly becoming poor after a few races. (For details of sailmaking in Terylene, see Appendix on page 126.)

Nylon

This is the forerunner of Terylene and has a similar appearance. It has, however, one disastrous property from a sailmaking point of view, this being a very great tendency to stretch. It is used only for spinnakers, for which it is excellent.

Sailcloth weights

In England, sailcloth, and canvas generally, is measured in ounces per square yard. Thus one yard of 36 in. 12 oz.

cloth would weigh exactly 12 oz. In America, on the other hand, the weight is taken in ounces per yard 28 in. wide, so that the same cloth is described as being 9 oz.

Dyeing and proofing (cotton)

The cloth may be coloured and/or proofed either in the bolt (roll) before the sail is made or after the sail is completed. Whatever the process, the canvas will tend to shrink, so that we would recommend that new sails should not be processed immediately after they are made, particularly as the shrinkage may be uneven. After the sail has been stretched to full size, dyeing will normally cause no harm, and the shrinkage should stretch out again without difficulty. There are three processes available: dyeing, mildew-proofing, and rendering water-repellent, the latter being recommended where it is desired to leave sails wet periodically. These processes are carried out by Sail Colour (Chichester) Ltd., Adelaide Road, Chichester, Sussex.

There are many firms, mostly in the North of England, who will dye sailcloth and canvas in the bolt, 300 linear yards of any one colour being the normal minimum, though lesser amounts may be dyed at an extra charge. Proofing can be done at the same time. Owing to the long run necessary for each colour, it is not normally practicable to have the cloth dyed specially for particular sails which are being ordered, but it may be that the sailmaker has some coloured cloth in stock which would be suitable. The dye itself is a hot vat dye and is as near fadeless as can be obtained.

Mildew-proofing is normally carried out on the cloth before the sail is made, and, though the stitching will not receive proofing, is to be recommended to avoid processing the sail as soon as it is made.

Dyeing and proofing (*Terylene*)

Terylene can be dyed in the piece to any shade, the dyes achieving a higher degree of light-fastness than cotton dyes. But, as yet, it does not appear practicable to dye finished sails, or short lengths of cloth.

Proofing is unncessary, though mildew- and water-repelling processes can be applied by the finishers.

How to obtain sailcloth

For small amounts we would recommend asking your sailmaker if he will supply you. W. G. Lucas & Son, of Broad Street, Portsmouth, Hants., a firm we have pleasure in recommending, have expressed their willingness to do so; and of course, our firm, Bowker & Budd Ltd., of Bosham, Sussex, will always be pleased to supply anything that may be required.

For greater lengths we would suggest contacting: Bowker & Budd Ltd., Bosham, Sussex; Lewis Clarke & Co. (London) Ltd., 2 Manor Lane, Holmes Chapel, Crewe, Cheshire; Howe & Bainbridge Inc., 220 Commercial Street, Boston 9, Mass., U.S.A.; Francis Webster & Sons Ltd., Alma Works, Arbroath, Scotland.

Estimating the amount of sailcloth required

Bermudian and gaff mainsails. Assuming the sides of the sail to be straight, calculate the area (using the fully stretched sizes) in square feet, add 25 per cent, and divide by 9 to bring to square yards. If 36 in. cloth is being used, this will give the yardage of the cloth required. Care should be taken to double the yardage if 18 in. cloths are to be used.

Foresails, staysails, jibs, genoas and topsails. Again assuming the sides to be straight and taking the fully stretched measurements, calculate the area in square feet and divide by 6. This gives the yardage required in cloth 36 in. wide, or half that needed in 18 in. cloth.

Note. The above formulae in most cases give the bare minimum of cloth required. If the order of laying the cloths is adhered to strictly, the amount will be sufficient. Otherwise a little more cloth may be needed to complete the job, as the wastage would be greater.

Parachute spinnakers. There is no very satisfactory rule of thumb in this case, as the wastage of cloth varies according to size, shape and cut. It is therefore best to make a scale drawing of half the spinnaker, marking in each cloth and totalling the yardage required (the cloth being laid full width). An approximate quantity, however, can be calculated by working out the finished area of the spinnaker in square feet and dividing by $5\frac{1}{2}$ to obtain the length of the cloth required in 36 in. wide; or more simply, multiply the luff by the foot in square feet, and divide by 7 to get the yardage in 36 in. wide.

If the sail plan shown in Chapter 7 is being used, this formula will be safe, though if the size of the sail happens to be an economical one, a few yards of cloth may be left over.

Stretching allowance

Best Egyptian cotton. The average amount which should be allowed for stretch would be 6 in. in 20 ft. If the material is cut on the cross the allowance should be doubled.

American cotton. This, of course, varies in accordance with the closeness of the weave, but on average would be 9 in. in 20 ft., or if cut on the cross, it would again be double.

R.N. flax. Here the allowances are approximately the

same as for American cotton, but as the material can stretch and contract more easily than cotton, it is safer to allow a little extra margin.

Terylene. With the latest heat set, high tenacity terylene, no stretching allowance is required, and the floor plan is drawn full-size.

Note. Although strictly speaking the same allowance should be made for the foot and the luff of a mainsail, both being cut on the cross, it is usual practice to make only half this allowance for the foot, owing to the greater difficulty in stretching the foot out. (For details of sailmaking in terylene, see Appendix, p. 126.)

Though allowance is made for the stretching of cotton sailcloth, it should be appreciated that the cotton does not in fact increase in area, but on the contrary tends to shrink; the shrinkage being considerable in cheaper and more loosely woven cloths. It is desirable, therefore, that the cloth should be pre-shrunk.

The apparent paradox of allowing for the stretching of a cloth which in fact shrinks is explained in this way: Where the cloth is cut on the cross, the edge will stretch automatically, taking the additional area required from other parts of the sail. If this stretch is not allowed for, the luff and foot will become too full. In the case of the leech of a mainsail, and leech and foot of a foresail, where the cloth is cut parallel or at right-angles to the weave, the additional strain placed on the tablings of the sail stretch the cloth at the expense of area elsewhere, though the stretch here is only approximately half that experienced by cloth cut on the cross.

Terylene on the other hand does not shrink, so that a sail in terylene to fit given spars will ordinarily, when in use, be slightly larger in area than the equivalent cotton sail, which, though stretching out to full length along the spars, will have shrunk in area.

*   *   *   *   *

RECOMMENDED WEIGHTS OF SAILCLOTH

Type of craft	Terylene or Best Egyptian cotton			R.N. flax	American cotton
Small dinghy - - -	3½	3½	2	—	4
10–14 ft. racing dinghy -	5	5	2	—	—
10–14 ft. sailing boats -	—	—	—	—	8
16–18 ft. racing dinghy -	7	5	2½	—	—
2½ ton cruiser - -	6	5	2½	7	8
National Swallow - -	7	5	2½	—	—
X class yacht - - -	8½	—	2½	—	—
International Dragon - -	8½	6	2½	—	—
4 ton cruising yacht - -	7	5	2½	—	9
6-Metre - - - -	11	8	2½	—	13
8-Metre - - -	13	9	3	—	15
6 ton cruiser - - -	8	6	2½	7	9
8 ton cruiser - - -	10	7	2½	5	12
10 ton cruiser - - -	11	8	2½	4	14
12 ton cruiser - - -	11	8	2½	4	14
15 ton cruiser - - -	15	11	3	3/4	21
20 ton cruiser - - -	18	12	3	3	—
30 ton cruiser - - -	21	15	3½	2	—

In the above table, the first column shows the weights of cloth recommended for mainsail and foresail, genoa and spinnaker respectively, in ounces per square yard. The second column shows the R.N. number of flax sailcloth. The third, the weights of American cotton in ounces per square yard for mainsail and foresail.

As already mentioned, America measures sailcloth in ounces per yard 28 in. wide. To find the American weight of a particular sailcloth, multiply, therefore by 4.

In each case, it is suggested that the foresail be the same weight as the mainsail. It may however, be slightly lighter, if preferred.

The table should be regarded as a guide only, as there may be occasions for varying the weights. In America, for instance, lighter weights are often preferred in parts where wind forces are generally less.

CHAPTER 3

SAILMAKING OPERATIONS

Machining

IT is usual in sailmaking to use a cross stitch machine (one that sews a zig-zag stitch) (Fig. 3), partly as the stitch looks better and partly as it allows the seam to stretch as far as it will. Sails can, and are, however, made satisfactorily with an ordinary straight stitch machine, domestic weight for smaller sails and tailor's weight for larger sizes.

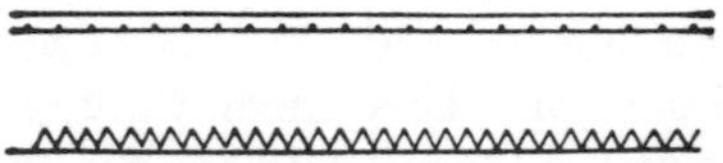

FIG. 3. Plan view of sail seam sewn on one side with straight stitch and the other with zig-zag stitch.

No special knowledge is required in the use of the machine, but it is desirable before starting on the actual sail to experiment with offcuts to make sure that you will be getting the stitch required. It will probably help to oil the machine first to ensure that it can cope with the long run of stitching. A sharp needle is a great help and it will probably pay to start off with a new one. There are two adjustments which come into play, that for regulating the tension to ensure that the knot of each stitch comes in the middle of the cloth rather than on the top or underneath and the control for altering the length of stitch.

Where a domestic machine is required to sew heaviet grades of cloth, the largest size needle should be fitted, and the heaviest gauge thread that the needle will take (to test this, take the needle out of the machine, thread it and place on the table with the groove downwards, the thread lying in the groove and coming up through the eye. Press the needle hard down on the table with the thumb on the centre of it, and if the thread can be drawn up through the eye it is not too thick. If it cannot be drawn up, the groove in the needle is too small and either a larger needle should be used, or a smaller size of thread). As the feed on a small machine will not draw heavier material through so efficiently it is best to help it by hand, using of course the longest stitch the machine can make.

For making false seams the initial row of stitching, in matching colour thread, should have long stitches, but the seam should be finished with stitches of medium length. Real seams should also have medium length stitches, as should also the rest of the sail with the exception of tabling edges where rope is to be sewn. Here the machining should be in as long stitches as possible, to keep the edge of the cloth pliable so that it will easily take the shape of the rope when this is sewn to the canvas. Where a cross stitch machine is used, the two halves of each stitch should be approximately at right angles, the stitch being lengthened as before where rope is to be sewn. Particular attention should be paid to the matching up of the strike-up marks (see Glossary).

For cotton and flax sails, a linen thread is best, this being chosen for its lasting qualities. It is usual, though not essential, to have a contrasting colour of thread to accentuate the position of the seams. Where straight stitching is used, it is often considered better to use a matching thread. Where the thread is coloured, this should be in a fast dye, as it is most objectionable if the colour runs into the surrounding cloth.

False-seaming (*cotton and flax only*)

So that the sail may maintain its shape, it is necessary that it be made up in comparatively narrow cloths, say 12 in. for small sails and 18 in. for larger ones. The cloth may sometimes be bought the correct width, but more often, particularly as it is more economical, the cloth is woven 36 in. wide.

Rather than cutting the cloth into the widths required, and seaming these together, a false seam is put in the

FIG. 4. Elevation view of a false seam, the vertical lines indicating the stitching.

cloth. When finished, this looks just like a real seam, and from end on, appears to resemble a flattened 'Z' (Fig. 4). The difference between the false and the real seams is that the first contains three thicknesses of cloths and the second only two (assuming that selvedge edges are employed in the real seam, which is normally the case).

To make the false seam, proceed as follows: If the cloths are to finish 12 in. wide and the cloth is 36 in., lay the cloth out on the floor and all the way along draw pencil lines exactly dividing the cloth into three equal strips Taking one first, bend the edge of the cloth downwards and under, so that the crease lies exactly along the pencil line. Now, the width of the seam in from the crease, sew a line of stitching (with straight stitch machine and colour the same as the cloth). Then take the other edge, bend downwards and under and sew in the same way.

Note. The false seams are always made the same width as the real ones in any one sail, and the width is usually as follows: For dinghies — $\frac{1}{2}$ in.; for $2\frac{1}{2}$-tonners and upwards — $\frac{3}{4}$ in.; for very large sails — 1 in.

When the material is laid out flat again, there will be two loops of cloth sticking up into the air. The cloth is laid on the sail plan in this condition, and as the cloths are sewn together, the false seams are sewn down by bending the loop one way or the other and flattening. The first row of stitching, being the same colour as the sail, will then not show at all. It is a matter of choice as to which way the false seam is sewn down, but all in any one sail should lay the same way.

The same procedure should be followed for other widths.

Handsewing

Sails are normally sewn partly by machine and partly by hand, the machine doing all that it can conveniently do, the rest being done by hand, with sailmaker's needle and palm, the latter being fitted with a metal pad positioned to lie in the palm of the hand. The needle is held between fingers and thumb with the eye on the pad, and so can be pushed hard without hurting the hand.

The normal sailmaker's needle is triangular, sizes 17 or 18 being suitable for dinghy sails, 15 and 16 for small yachts and 14 or 14$\frac{1}{2}$ for larger sails. For all cotton sails, a three-cord reverse twist linen thread is recommended. The size of the thread varies according to the job in hand, but in general, as small a size as will give adequate strength for the particular sail should be used. If in doubt it would be better to err on the larger side, but if the thread when pulled tight after the stitch, tears the canvas before breaking, then the thread chosen is too strong. The same needle is used for roping, except that in this case the point is dulled.

In nylon and terylene sails, it is best to use only synthetic threads, but if need be there would be no harm in using linen or cotton. The effect in this case would merely be that the thread would form much the weakest part of the sail, not only because it would be weaker but also as it would not last so long.

The following points apply to all handsewing: (1) Do not knot the thread except for roping. (2) Use the thread double normally, but use four parts for heavy jobs. (3) Wax the thread well with beeswax. (4) As you sew, twist the needle anti-clockwise (as you look at the point). These turns will be taken out automatically in the process of sewing, and will thus prevent the thread becoming twisted. (5) Start by leaving a spare $1\frac{1}{2}$ in. or so at the end of the thread, and sew this end in as you proceed. (6) Finish by going over the last stitch twice and then run the thread between the two parts of cloth, making it reappear about 2 in. away, where it is cut off.

Flat seaming for hand sewing seams of sails, fitting patches, etc., where the machine cannot reach easily. This stitch is carried out entirely on the top side of the cloth. With needle and palm, start by pressing the needle down through the sail, bringing the point straight up again in one operation so that it comes up through the edge of the patch. Pull tight and repeat the process a little further along the seam to be sewn. On average, the stitches should be about five to the inch, and should appear to move forward on the top and be at right angles to the seam underneath.

c

Round seaming, for oversewing the edges of two cloths together (used, in best quality work, along the leading edge of wire luff headsails, the tabling having been cut and re-sewn. Also very largely in general canvas work, such as fendoffs, etc.) Start by pressing the needle through the two parts of the cloth away from you and close to the edge of the cloth. Return over the outside of the edge of the cloth and repeat, placing the next stitch close to the first, the distance between being about the thickness of the thread.

Sticking stitch, used largely for securing a luff wire by sewing as close to the wire as possible on the inboard side of the wire. Pass the needle through the cloth away from you, at an angle, so that the point is proceeding in the direction of stitching. Move forward a little way (say $\frac{1}{8}$ in.) and return through the cloth in the same way, again inclining the point in the direction of stitching. Again stitch away from you in the same way and so on. The result is that a little stitch is visible at longer intervals either side, most of the progression having been carried out actually inside the canvas. The running stitch is the same except that the needle is inserted in each case at right angles to the cloth.

Roping (Plate I)

This operation consists of sewing the bolt rope to the edge of the sail. The rope should be Italian hemp (or terylene for terylene sails) for most ordinary sails, and the following sizes are usually chosen for modern craft:

For sail area of

up to 30 sq. ft.	-	-	$\frac{1}{2}$ in. circumference
30 sq. ft. to 100 sq. ft.	-	-	$\frac{3}{4}$ in. circumference
100 sq. ft. to 150 sq. ft.	-	-	$\frac{7}{8}$ in. circumference

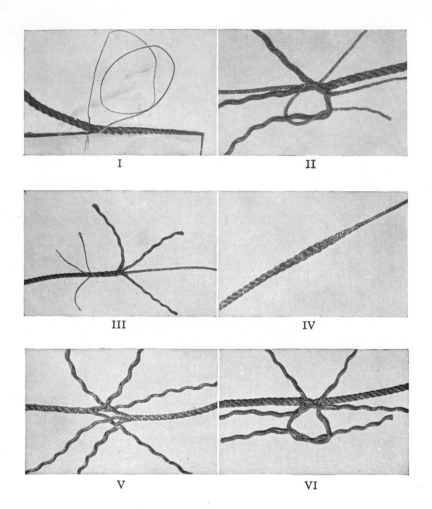

I

II

III

IV

V

VI

150 sq. ft. to 200 sq. ft. -   - 1 in. circumference
200 sq. ft. to 300 sq. ft. -   - $1\frac{1}{4}$ in. circumference
          Over 300 sq. ft. -   - $1\frac{1}{2}$ in. circumference

In the old days there was a tendency to fit larger ropes than is usual today, partly due to the fact that the vessels were generally heavier and stiffer, requiring stronger sails. In such cases, a size larger bolt rope should be fitted.

Note. Rope is sold by the pound rather than by length so that all rope of a particular type can be the same price, and is measured by circumference rather than diameter as it is difficult to measure a true diameter.

The principle of roping is to pass the thread through the lay of the rope using a dull pointed needle to assist in passing cleanly between the strands without picking up odd fibres from one of them, and stitching to the edge of the sail so that the thread passes round one strand only, leaving the other two outside it. The rope is always sewn to the port side to assist in identifying by feel the part of the sail being held. And as the rope stretches more than the canvas, allowance for this is made in each stitch.

The roping of a sail is carried out as follows:

Note. The measurements which follow apply to sails of about 150 sq. ft. For larger sails they should be scaled up in proportion.

First make a tail on one of the ropes in this manner: bind the rope at a point 9 in. from the end. Unlay the strands and then, taking each strand separately, unlay completely so that each strand becomes a bunch of fibres. With a sharp knife, shave the fibres down between the thumb and the blade, taking small quantities of the fibres at a time (it will usually be convenient to divide the fibres into about 12 lots). Now take the seizing and wax the tail thoroughly. Divide the fibres into three separate strands, and lay up two strands by twisting each strand the *opposite* way from the way you are laying the two strands up. Having come to a fine point, lay the third strand in the same way. You should now have a rope evenly tapering to a point. (We would recommend practising first on a spare piece of rope).

The rope should be marked with a guide line as follows: take the turns out of the rope so that it is in a completely relaxed state — i.e. not wanting to turn either way — stretch tight and mark a line on it all the way down. This line should not be allowed to deviate from the edge of the leech. Care has to be taken to prevent this, as the tendency is for the line to move round the rope as you stitch.

Start roping at a point 3 in. up the leech from the top of the clew liner (this is the long patch running up the leech from the clew of a mainsail). Take a chair without arms and place it so that there is a heavy table or other fixed object a few feet away on the right hand side of the chair. Attach the sail hook, which is a small metal hook with a sharp point, to a piece of line, and attach the other end of the line to a fixed object, such as a table leg, a few feet to your right (professional sailmakers use a specially designed bench, the sail hook attaching at one end, and of sufficient length to enable him to slide conveniently along it as the roping proceeds). Now sit, and place the leech of the sail on your lap with the clew liner uppermost. Turn the leech of the sail upwards, and place the rope on the edge of the leech on the side nearest your body, with the point of the tail 3 in. up the leech from the top of the clew liner.

With needle and palm, and hand thread (waxed), over-sew the point of the tail to the leech for ½ in., after which the rope must be sewn as follows: Insert the needle

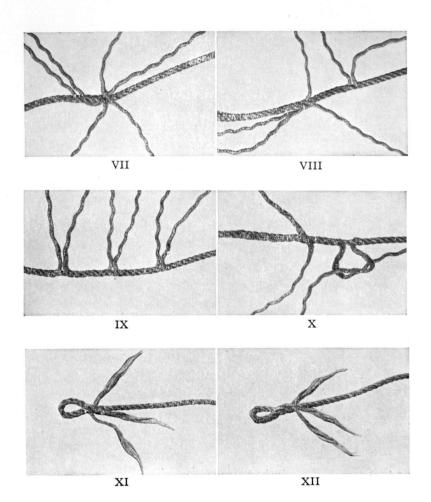

VII VIII

IX X

XI XII

PLATES VII–XII

through the rope (pointing away from you), so that it goes cleanly between the strands, leaving two strands below and one above the needle (care must be taken that the needle does not catch any of the fibres of the strands, and to help in this it is desirable that the needle should not be too sharp). Keeping the rope carefully in position, press the needle through the sail, and pull the thread tight to the *left*. Now insert the needle in the same way through the next lay, and so on all the way. To stop the guide line on the rope from moving away from the edge of the sail, take a turn out of the rope with the right hand after every few stitches.

As the rope stretches more than the canvas, it is necessary to take in a little more canvas to each stitch, and instead of pressing the needle through the rope at right angles to the sail, place the needle through the rope and move the point to the right a little before pushing it through the canvas, thereby taking in a little more canvas. (Again we advise practising on a spare piece of rope and a piece of cloth.) During this operation the sail hook will have been placed in the clew eyelet, and the sail pulled tight with the left hand so that the edge of the sail is tight while being roped.

Having reached the clew, preparations for roping the foot must be made before proceeding. Fasten the free end of the rope to a fixed object and, holding it at the clew, stretch the rope as tight as you can. Now lay the foot of the sail along the rope, tight but not stretched, in such a way that the guide line runs along the edge of the canvas. At foot intervals, fix the rope to the sail (through the lay of the rope) with a temporary lashing. When the rope is freed off, it will be seen that the length of canvas taken is a little more than the length of the rope.

Continue roping along the foot in the same manner as before, making sure that you take in the extra canvas with each stitch, so that as each temporary lashing is reached you do not get a pucker in the cloth. Remove the temporary lashings as you get to them. When you reach the tack, stretch the rope and fix to the luff at foot intervals in the same way and rope all the way up the luff. On reaching the headboard, sew strongly over the rope through the same holes in the headboard. Continue round the headboard, and continue roping down the leech. Make another tail as before, so that the point lies 6 in. below the bottom of the head patch.

When roping a splice, or at a point where extra strength is required, a double stitch should be made. Having passed the needle through the rope and the sail, pass the thread back over the rope and sew again through the same hole on the rope side, but making the point of the needle emerge about $\frac{1}{16}$ in. further along the sail. Then carry on in the normal way, doing another double stitch as required. The appearance of this double stitch is an uneven zig-zag. To indicate where double stitching is desirable it is safe to say that it may be used wherever additional patches are sewn to the sail.

In roping large sails, it is desirable to obtain extra pull by winding the thread a few times round a wooden handle, and then rolling the handle.

Tapered splice (Plates II-IV)

For joining ropes of different sizes. Mate the two ends together so that each strand of one part lies between two of the other part. Without altering the position, it will be seen that each strand of one rope will come opposite to one of the other rope. Tie each pair together with an overhand

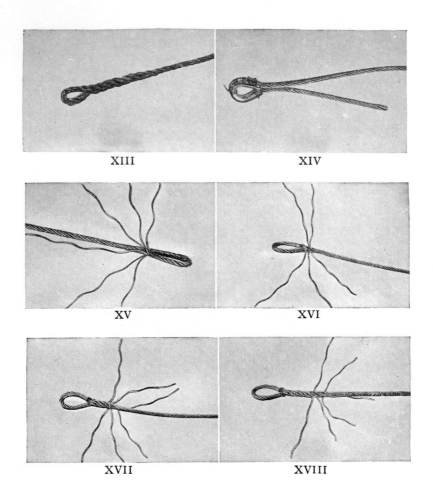

XIII

XIV

XV

XVI

XVII

XVIII

PLATES XIII–XVIII

knot, all the three knots to be tied the same way, i.e. starting each knot with the strand from the right hand rope behind the strand from the left-hand rope. Tuck away from the join in both directions as for an eye splice, the unlaying of each strand ensuring that the splice does not finish appreciably thicker than the thicker rope. After the second and subsequent tucks, cut away one sixth of the total number of fibres from each strand.

Long splice (Plates V-X)

For joining equal ropes, so that the diameter at the join is not increased. Mate up as for a tapered splice and place a seizing one side of the join and close to it, leaving out one of the strands of the other rope (the seizing can be conveniently made just by tying a clove hitch with the sewing twine) so that the seizing is round the right hand rope and also includes two strands of the left hand rope. The one strand from the left hand rope which has been left out of the seizing will be opposite one of the strands of the right hand rope. This latter strand should be unlayed from the right hand rope, a turn at a time, and its opposite number laid into the rope instead, tightening up the strand as you lay it in, for a distance of about 12 in. (more for larger ropes). Knot the two ends together with an overhand knot, as in the tapered splice, and, unlaying each strand, tuck it across the lay over one and under two, cutting off the ends.

Now remove the seizing, and taking two opposite strands, proceed in exactly the same way the opposite way for the same distance, finishing off as before. This leaves two strands in the middle. These are knotted with an overhand knot, starting with the right hand strand behind the left-hand one as in the tapered splice, unlaying the strands

and tucking each over one and under two across the lay
Cut off the ends and the splice is finished.

Rope eye-splice (Plates XI–XIII)

Unlike the normal rope splice, where each strand is
tucked across the lay of the rope, the sailmaker's splice is
tucked with the lay so that the splice can be roped to the
sail with the rest of the rope. Start by opening the three
strands, for the eye the size required, and place the unlayed strands evenly over the rope. With the eye towards
you, lift one strand of the rope (twist the rope to open the
strands a little), tuck from left to right. Next lift the strand
to the right of the first strand lifted, and tuck under it,
again from left to right, the strand to the right of the one
first tucked. Tuck the remaining strand similarly under
the strand on the left of the one first lifted.

Taking each strand in turn, unlay so that the strand
consists of a bunch of fibres, pass over the strand of the
rope which lies on the left, lift this strand and tuck under
from left to right. Tuck the other two strands similarly.
The purpose of unlaying each strand before tucking is so
that it lays in the rope much more evenly and smoothly.
Having completed the second tuck, cut from each strand
one-sixth the number of fibres, and make the third tuck
Then cut away the same number of fibres in each case and
make the fourth tuck and so on until the splice is finished.
If preferred, a tail can be made at the end of the rope (see
page 23) and the rope tucked until the point of the tail is
reached. In each case the ends should finish in line along
the rope. It is best to sew the rope to the sail before cutting
the ends off, in order to make sure that they are sewn in
properly.

Wire eye-splice (Plates XIV–XVIII)

There are a number of ways of making this splice, all of which are satisfactory, but the most convenient, and the one that can most easily be made neat, is that tucked with the lay in the same way as the rope eye-splice. First mark the place where the wire is to be cut, leaving at least 12 in. for the splice (more for large wires). Heat the wire locally at this point with a flame until it is red hot. Allow to cool and cut at the same point with a cold chisel. In this way the wire can be cut without the strands separating until desired, and without each strand unravelling when separated. If a flame is not available, each strand can be whipped.

Place the wire round the thimble in the required position and mark with pencil the two parts at positions exactly level with the point of the thimble. Remove the thimble, and holding the wire looped in the same position, bind the two parts together very tightly, starting at the marks and working towards the loop. (Care should always be taken to make the loop of the splice smaller rather than larger than the correct size as the loop can always be enlarged with a fid, but cannot be made smaller without resplicing). The wire is now ready for the tucks.

Place the wire in a vice at a position about 2 ft. from the loop. Holding the loop towards you, spread out the six strands so that they lie evenly over the other part of the wire, three strands lying to the right and three to the left. Cut out the centre strand. Place a bar through the loop and twist anti-clockwise to facilitate lifting the strands of the wire. Take the right hand loose strand, lift with a spike two of the strands which lie opposite to it, and tuck under these two from left to right. Next lift the left hand of the two previously lifted, and tuck number two strand under it from left to right. Lift the next strand to the left, and tuck number three similarly and so on until all six strands have been tucked. After each strand has been tucked, it should be pulled back towards the loop and given a right hand half turn with a pair of pliers to make it lay into the wire.

The second tuck is carried out in exactly the same way, each strand in this case laying over one and under one, all from left to right, so that each strand passes over and then under the same strand beneath which it passed in the first tuck. The third tuck is completed in the same way. In the fourth tuck only alternate strands are tucked, each of these laying over one and under two strands. After the second, third and fourth tucks, the splice should be smoothed off with a hammer before the ends are cut off. Cut the ends as close to the wire as possible, ensuring that all the burnt parts of the wire are removed as these would rust more quickly. Cover the splice with canvas to prevent the loose ends projecting through the sail before sewing the wire into the sail.

The thimble is knocked into position with a mallet after the loop of wire has been sewn into position. Where the eye projects beyond the corner of the sail, the wire of the loop should be served with marline before the splice is made, and in this case, the thimble is spliced into position.

The following table will serve as a guide in choosing a suitable size of wire:

For sail with luff
up to 12 ft.	-	- $\frac{1}{2}$ in. circumference
from 12 ft.–25 ft.	-	- $\frac{3}{4}$ in. circumference
from 25 ft.–35 ft.	-	- $\frac{7}{8}$ in. circumference
from 35 ft.–40 ft.	-	- 1 in. circumference

These sizes would be suitable for modern yacht sails,

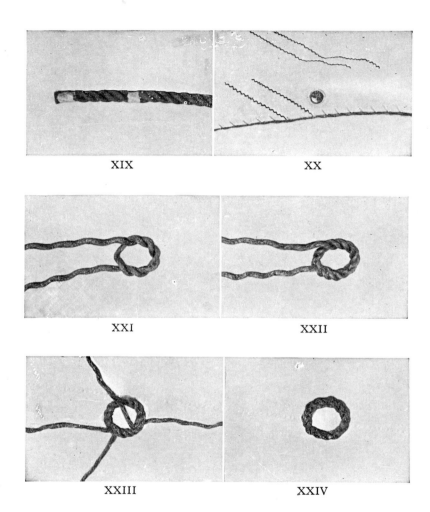

XIX   XX

XXI   XXII

XXIII   XXIV

PLATES XIX–XXIV

but can be varied as required. For storm jibs, sails on heavy gaff-rigged vessels, etc., larger sizes would be desirable.

Normally, flexible galvanised wire is used, but the same size of stainless steel can be used in preference. Phosphor-bronze is also sometimes used, but is not recommended owing to lesser strength.

Where Wykeham-Martin furling gear is fitted, head-sails are sometimes fitted with a luff galvanised chain to ensure that the head will roll equally with the tack. The chain should be small in size, having links with as small internal size as possible.

Wire-to-rope-splice

This is not often used, but may be required where a mainsail has a wire luff and a leech tail rope from the headboard down the leech. It is carried out in exactly the same way as a tapered rope splice, dividing the six strands of the wire into pairs. To bind the splice the three rope strands are tucked first under two wire strands in each case, but in the second tuck, they each pass again under two wire strands but this time the three pairs of wire strands are so arranged that the gaps between them occur between the two strands that made up the previous pairs, the third tuck again taking the original pairs. The splice should be placed so that its centre lies on the top of the headboard. Back-splice the loose wire ends for two tucks and serve the whole splice.

Sailmaker's whipping (Plate XIX)

This is very easily carried out with needle and hand-thread, used double. First pass the needle through the lay of the rope, leaving one strand one side of the needle and two the other. Wind the thread round the rope as tightly as possible ensuring that the two parts of the thread do not cross each other, for as long as is desired (say for the distance of the diameter of the rope). Then pass the needle through the lay again, as before, (it does not matter which side of the needle the single thread lies). Having pulled the thread tight through the rope, follow the lay of the strands across the whipping, and insert the needle through the lay in the same way, and pull tight (the two threads now lying across the whipping should be lying snugly in the groove between two of the strands of rope). Again follow the lay and insert the needle at the other end of the whipping between the strands, bringing the point out in the free position, i.e., the position not already filled by the previous two strands of thread. Follow the lay again and again pass the needle through the rope.

This completes the whipping and it only remains to finish it off. It is desirable to start the whipping on the inboard end of the rope and finish it here also. The whipping may be finished in any way, but a good way is to sew round two strands separately, so that the thread looks like part of the whipping. The end should then be cut off. Having finished the whipping, the rope should be cut neatly and close to it (say $\frac{1}{4}$ in. from it). For safety a second whipping should be placed a few inches further up the rope.

Sewn eyelet (Plate XX)

The object of sewing in an eyelet is to give it maximum strength. First place the ring in the appropriate position on the sail and draw round its inside with pencil. Then make a round hole in the cloth with diameter half that of the inside of the ring. With needle and palm sew the ring

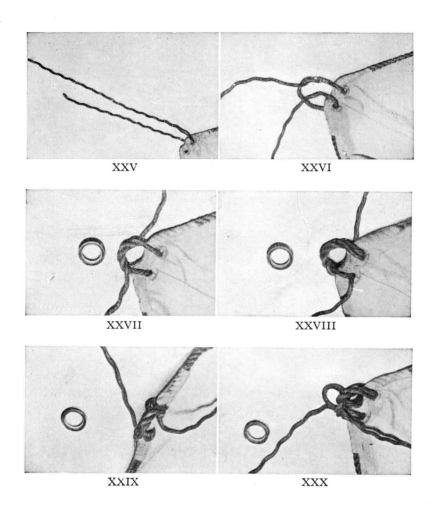

XXV

XXVI

XXVII

XXVIII

XXIX

XXX

PLATES XXV–XXX

to the sail, round and round the metal of the ring, each stitch lying as close as possible to the last, and the same size.

The eyelet as it now stands is quite satisfactory, but to avoid chafe, a brass thimble should be punched into the eyelet, by inserting the thimble, which is specially shaped, into the hole and splaying it out to the shape of an ordinary thimble with a special punch and die.

Grommet (Plates XXI–XXIV)

This consists of a ring of rope. Take one strand from a piece of rope. Take the two ends, both pointing upwards, cross the right hand one behind the left, and lay up the right hand end round the left, twisting the strand tight as you go. Proceed round again so that the ring now looks like a continuous ring of new rope. The two ends will now be opposite to each other. Tie them together with an overhand knot (right hand strand being placed first behind the left hand one), having unlaid the strands. Finish each end as in the long splice by crossing the lay, over one and under two, remembering to unlay the strands before tucking so that they lay in properly. Fid out the grommet tightly before cutting the ends off. A wire grommet is made in the same way, except that six turns will be required.

Cringle (Plates XXV–XXXIII)

This consists of a loop of rope on the edge of a sail, holding a round thimble tightly. Again it is made from a single strand of rope, and in order to calculate before hand how much rope is required, count along the new rope (before the strands are separated) 64 lays. This will give the correct length for whatever the size of rope.

Whip both ends of the strand first (sellotape may be used conveniently). With the bolt rope towards you and the sail away from you, take one end and pass through the left eyelet in the tabling; hold the two parts together in such a way that the top part is one third as long again as the lower. Starting at the bolt rope, lay up the two parts for three complete turns (that is, crossing the strand three times). Pass the longer end up through the right hand eyelet and down between the bolt rope and cringle rope, laying this strand with its own part in a natural position for one turn only.

Next place the thimble over the grommet, so that the inside edge of the thimble is immediately over the outside edge of the bolt rope. If the cringle is the correct size to fit the thimble, the inside should come exactly under the centre of the thimble. If it does not, the long strand should be loosened or tightened until it does. With the long strand, continue round the lay and down through the left hand eyelet on the outside of the strand already there. Pass the shorter end up through the right hand eyelet so that this also lies outside the strand already there. (If the cringle is formed correctly, these two strands will lie naturally in these positions. If they do not, it may be because more or less than three turns were taken in the first place.)

Now lift the bolt rope and lay the sail the reverse way so that the canvas is the other way up and the bolt rope is away from you. Take the left hand strand and place downwards between the strands of the cringle, touching the bolt rope and at the left hand eyelet, so that the two strands of the cringle lie to the left and one to the right. Lift the bolt rope so that the cringle points upwards, and turn the sail round so that you look at the other side of the

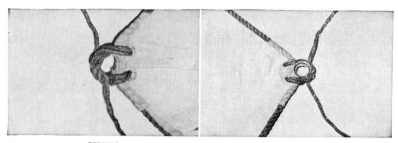

XXXI   XXXII

XXXIII

cringle, and carry out exactly the same procedure with the other strand.

With the cringle placed either way, take the left hand strand, pick up with the spike the strand of the cringle immediately on its right, unlay the left hand strand and pass through the lifted strand towards you. Pull tight in such a way that this strand and the one beneath which it has passed appear to fuse together to make one strand. Finish the strand by crossing the lay over one and under two, having again unlaid the strand. Again turn the sail and proceed in exactly the same way for the other strand. (The finishing of the second strand will in fact cross the first, but as both have been unlaid and fused into the strands of the cringle, this presents no difficulty.)

The cringle is now complete and ready for the thimble to be fitted. Take a piece of twine exactly the same length of $3\frac{1}{7}$ times the outside diameter of the thimble, hold the twine in a loop so that the two ends just touch, and pass the loop over the point of the fid. Slide the loop down the fid until it fits tightly round it. Mark this point on the fid with chalk. With the bolt rope on the lower side of the sail and the fid pointing upwards, place the cringle over the fid point and knock down with a wooden mallet (place old canvas over the sail to prevent damage) until the cringle reaches the chalk mark. Leave the cringle in this position for five minutes.

Speed in the next part of the operation is essential. Have your thimble ready, mallet in hand; with the fid pointing downwards, knock the cringle down the fid, throw the fid aside, place the thimble on the cringle, the outside edge of the thimble being placed in position inside the rope of the cringle. Hit the inside edge of the thimble with the mallet so that this also fits in. The thimble should now be tight, between the bolt rope and the cringle rope. Very high speed is necessary in this operation. If you find you cannot get the thimble into the cringle, fid it out again in the same way and carry out the operation again (it may take a little practice before sufficient speed can be achieved) If some strands are not set in the thimble, these should be eased in with a spike. The speed, of course, is necessary as the thimble must be inserted before the cringle has time to contract again after being removed from the fid.

Lastly, with the cringle pointing upwards, lift one loose end and place the fid behind it (near the point). Pass the end completely round the fid; hold it tight on the fid with one hand and turn the fid with the other in a clockwise direction, tightening up the strand, and continue turning until the strand breaks off clean (failing this, the strand may be cut off). Finish the other loose end in the same way. Wax the cringle to protect it from the weather. If it is properly tight, a metallic sound may be obtained from the thimble by hitting the outside of the cringle rope. (*Note.* For strength, the cringle is usually formed over the bolt rope and through two sewn eyelets.)

Drawing a straight line in chalk

First chalk a length of thin cotton line, stretch it tightly and securely along the line required to be drawn on the floor, lift the cotton at a point near one end and allow to drop sharply. The impact will shake the chalk from the cotton to leave a perfectly straight line.

CHAPTER 4

THE FORESAIL, JIB, STAYSAIL AND GENOA

ALTHOUGH headsails vary considerably in shape and style, they fall into three main categories. First the jib, a fairly narrow sail, with the clew cut high, and with long luff, incorporating jib topsails, yankees, etc., second the staysail, with shorter luff and usually with the angle at the clew somewhere near 90°; and third the genoa, being low-cut and with a very long foot. Except for minor differences, the construction of all these sails is the same, so that for general principles they can all be considered together.

Essentially, the headsail is a three-sided sail, stretched tight along the luff, which is fitted with either wire or rope, the leech and foot being unsupported. Bearing in mind that the weave of the cloth must be parallel or at right angles to the unsupported sides, it will be seen that there are three possible methods of arranging the cloth. First, the mitre cut (Fig. 5A), the most commonly used method, where the seams cut both the foot and leech at right angles, meeting on the last seam, which bisects the clew (to avoid creases in the cloth, it is necessary to ensure that the seams meet each other on the last seam exactly); the next arrangement applies only to sails where the clew is exactly 90°, as the cloths are laid vertically, and parallel to the leech, so that they cut the foot at right angles (Fig. 5B) — the advantage of this being merely that it is cheaper and easier; and the third arrangement, the Scotch cut, is the same as the mitre except that the cloths lie parallel to the leech and foot (Fig. 5c). Again the only value is financial, as undoubtedly this cut does not set so well as the mitre, the seams joining the cloths tending to protrude.

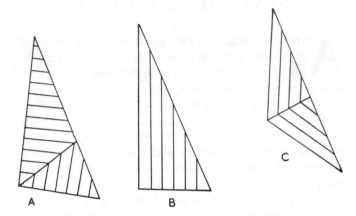

FIG. 5. (A) Mitre cut; (B) Vertical cut; (C) Scotch cut.

To achieve maximum driving power from the headsail, it is of course necessary to make it as full as possible for the particular point of sailing. As it is not possible to adjust the fullness, this naturally boils down to making the sail as full as will set when the yacht is lying as near the wind as she will for best results. (It is not easy to establish what angle from the wind this exactly is, but for the average boat, it is likely to be near 45°, fast racing boats being less and heavier types more. Care should be taken to avoid supposing that the yacht is necessarily sailing best to windward when she is pointing as well as she can, as the ability of a yacht to point is purely dependent on how flat the sails are.)

Having determined how full the sail should be, the next step is to design the sail so that, when set, it will have just this amount of fullness. This presents a difficulty as the stronger the wind blowing on any given sail, the fuller will the sail be, merely because the cloth stretches. Thus for best results, it is necessary to have two or more sails, all the same size, but graded for use in different wind forces by the amount of fullness. The resulting large wardrobe of sails, though highly desirable for the racing yacht, would be expensive and a nuisance for the average cruiser, so generally a sail of average fullness is used, one which constitutes the best compromise, and it is the making of this with which the second half of this chapter deals.

The method of imparting fullness to the sail is extremely simple. When the plan is drawn on the floor, the luff is cut as a convex curve, and in due course, the luff wire is fitted along this curve. As soon as the sail is set, and the luff wire is pulled out straight, the surplus cloth goes into the sail (one of the reasons why it is so necessary to keep the forestay, and the headsail luff, really tight, is to prevent further fullness being imparted to the sail by the luff being allowed to sag). As the majority of the sail area is below the halfway mark of the luff, the maximum depth of the convex curve will also be below, and is in fact usually two-thirds of the way down, and the amount of fullness required for a particular sail is controlled purely by the depth given to the curve.

Although Genoas are mitre cut on the same principle as other headsails, it is necessary to treat them with special care, owing to the great length of foot which tends to exaggerate any slight faults there might be. Added to this is the necessity of allowing for the stretching of the last seam bisecting the clew. It is natural to expect this seam to stretch as it cuts all the cloths at a considerable angle. On the average headsail, where the last seam is short, the stretch can be disregarded, but in a Genoa this is not so, and the effect of the stretch is to make the sail fuller, not only from forward to aft, but up and down as well. The foot and leech, being at right angles to the weave, stretch little, and the luff, being wired, does not stretch at all, so that if the seam across the middle stretches, the sail will tend to become bowl-shaped, which is a shape only suitable for running.

If, however, the foot and leech were allowed to stretch along with the last seam, this trouble would not arise, as the main body of the sail, the part, that is, which is clear of the fullness imparted at the luff, would remain flat; and this is achieved by allowing the cloths to cut the leech and foot at an angle slightly less than 90°, (Fig. 6). The cloth now being cut slightly on the cross will stretch just a little, and to make a really good Genoa, this angle must be exactly right.

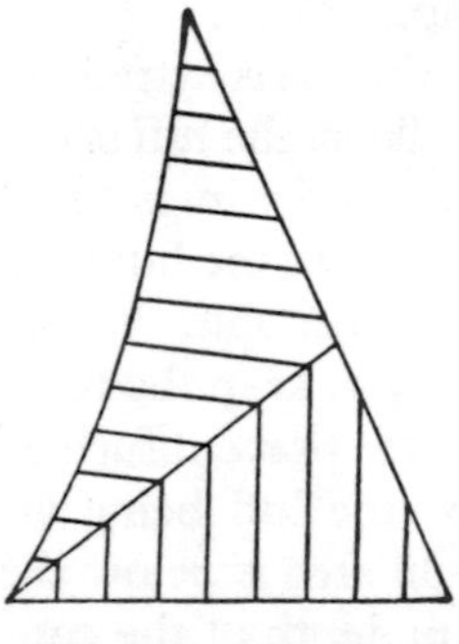

FIG. 6 Mitre cut Genoa, showing the angle of cloths to leech and foot slightly off-set.

But there is more to it than this. In order to make the leech set properly without flapping or curling over, it is essential to cut it with a substantial concave curve. This means that the lower half of the leech is cut more on the cross than the foot, which is cut with only a slight convex curve, and that, per foot, the leech will stretch slightly more than the foot. This can of course be corrected by making the angle of the cloth to the leech (that is, the straight line joining the head and clew) a little less. But, and this is important, the angles of the top and lower halves of the sail meeting the last seam, must be the same, to enable each seam to meet its opposite number. If the angle at the leech is altered, the angle at the last seam must change too, which would mean changing the angle of the cloths to the foot. Thus the only way of altering the angle at the leech in relation to that at the foot would be to move the last seam.

We think that the foregoing, together with relevant information on the cloth itself, should provide the data an expert mathematician would need for calculating exactly how to lay the cloths, but luckily for most of us it works out very much more simply in practice. The last seam does in fact bisect the clew, but using the straight line of the leech, rather than the concave curve, so that in the actual sail it appears to be above the bisection point. Next one must mark in on the floor plan the hollow curve of the leech, and the depth of this may be calculated from the accompanying graph. For instance, if the luff is 32 ft. and the last seam is half as long as the luff, then the depth of the hollow will be 9 in. The hollow is drawn in as a perfectly regular curve. Where the last seam is only one quarter, or less, of the luff, the curve is nil and coincides with the straight line of the plan.

Now to find the angle the cloths should make to the straight lines of the leech and foot, measure down the leech one-sixth of the distance, and at this point, draw a line at right angles to the curved line of the leech, cutting the straight line of the leech and the luff. All the cloths in the upper part of the sail will lie parallel to this line, and those in the lower part are also fixed, as they must strike the last seam at the same angle.

It will be appreciated that this method of calculating the lay is the outcome of experience, rather than theoretical reasoning, the method having been evolved from what was found to be desirable in practice. Minor variations may be found in other sails, but if our system is followed exactly, the results are certain to give satisfaction.

For a fuller appreciation of Genoas, we feel that it is worth mentioning the older method of dealing with the same problem. In the past it was a firm rule that in head-sails of all sorts the cloths must strike the leech and foot at right angles, and, instead of allowing the foot and leech to stretch with the last seam, the last seam itself was made shorter to begin with, so that by the time it had stretched it was the correct length in comparison with leech and foot. This was done by making each seam, as it approached the last seam, a little wider, by giving the cloth slightly larger overlaps, and thereby making each cloth a little nar-rower. The result of this was that when the sail was new, the last seam would stand out slightly from the body of the sail in the form of a low ridge, which gradually disappeared as the last seam stretched. The disadvantages of this method lay in the facts that it was much more tricky to ensure that the sails would be exactly right when stretched, and that more work was involved in making the sail.

In the actual manufacture of the sail, it is desirable to make the luff tabling a generous width, and this should be cut from the sail and sewn to it the same way up, so that the weave in the tabling matches that in the sail (if the tabling is formed merely by turning the edge of the sail over, the weave would not match, the luff being cut on the cross, and wrinkles would result). The tabling, after being cut, should also be moved along the luff a few inches so that the seams in the tabling no longer coincide with those in the sail.

For ordinary foresails, where the cloths strike the leech and foot at right angles, the tablings on these sides may be formed by turning over the edge of the cloth, but in genoa leeches the hollow causes the cloth to be cut slightly on the cross, and the tabling should be cut and resewn. In this case, allowance must be made for the fact that the tabling, being double thickness of cloth, will stretch less than the sail itself, by sewing, say, $12\frac{1}{8}$ in. of tabling on to every 12 in. of cloth.

The patches at the corners should not be skimped, and should be more comprehensive as the sail gets larger. These, together with the under patches, are fitted so that there is stitching on the edge of the patch only, allowing a certain amount of independent movement between the sail and the patch. The clew, head and tack thimbles are usually fitted as extensions to the sail, but where, for racing, it is desirable to obtain maximum area within the measurements, these may all be found fitted within the triangle formed by the sailcloth.

Occasionally it is desirable to fit a foresail with reef points; for this we would refer you to the section of Chapter 6 which deals with reef points in mainsails, as the principle is just the same.

The manufacture is carried out in various stages, and for the normal headsail is as follows:

Tools required

Wire spike, needles, wax, chalk, palm, string and tape, sail hook, mallet and hammer, sharp knife.

Operation 1 Drawing the sail plan, which is a drawing

on a floor the actual size and shape of a sail before stretching (see Chapter 2 for stretching allowances) (Fig. 7). Choose, if possible, a wooden floor into which prickers may be pressed, though any other floor of sufficient size may be used. Having calculated the unstretched measure-

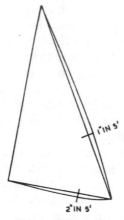

ments of the sail, draw these as straight lines on the floor with chalk, the resulting figure being a triangle. In the actual sail, the leech remains straight but the luff and foot curve outwards. Mark in these curves as follows:

Luff — measure from the tack one-third of the length of luff, and at this point measure outwards from the luff 1 in. for every 5 ft. of luff (i.e. for a luff of 15 ft. measure outwards 3 in.). Using a tape-measure, or something simi-lar, join the tack and head by a smooth curve passing through this point. To see if the curve is correct

Fig. 7. Floor plan of the foresail.

and fair, place the eye near the floor at one end and look along the curve, when irregularities will immediately be apparent. Move the tape until the curve is satisfactory, and then mark the curve on the floor with chalk.

Foot — measure from the tack one-third of the length of the foot, and at this point measure outwards 2 in. for every 5 ft. length of foot. Join the tack and clew by a smooth curve passing through this point in the same way (Fig. 7). Now bisect exactly the clew angle, so that the bisecting line cuts the curved line of the luff. This line represents the last seam.

Operation 2 False seaming the cloth. Sailcloth can be obtained especially woven 1 ft. or 18 in. wide, but usually, for economy, it is woven 36 in. wide (or more), and as narrow cloths are essential, false seams are sewn into the sails (when the sail is finished, these are indistinguishable from real seams, and in fact are just as good). Normally the cloths are required to be 12 in. apart, so that if the material is 36 in. wide, two false seams are sewn in, in the following manner.

Lay the cloth on the floor and, with pencil, draw two lines the whole length dividing the cloth exactly into three lengths 12 in. wide. Take one line first, bend the edge of the cloth downwards and under, so that the crease lies exactly along the pencil line. Now, exactly $\frac{1}{2}$ in. in from the crease, sew a line of stitching. Do the same to the other pencil line, and then lay the cloth out flat on the floor again when it will, end on, look like Fig. 4.

The widths of both real and false seams are usually $\frac{1}{2}$ in. for dinghies, $\frac{3}{4}$ in. for $2\frac{1}{2}$-tonners and upwards, and 1 in. for large sails.

The cloth is now ready for laying on the plan (the false seams being completed at a later stage).

Operation 3 Laying the cloth on the plan. First measure the exact width of the cloth (this will now be a little less than 36 in.) and then, from the clew of the plan, measure along both the leech and the foot, this amount. From the points obtained, exactly at right angles to the leech and foot, draw lines which should meet on the last seam line.

Start laying the cloth for the lower half of the sail, (Fig. 8). With the false seam upwards, lay the first cloth with the edge overlapping the foot by $1\frac{1}{2}$ in. (make sure first that the end of the cloth is at right angles to the sides), so that the edge of the cloth lies along the line just drawn at right angles to the foot. Use prickers to hold the cloth in position, or if the floor is not suitable, use weights. Cut the cloth so that there remains an overlap of $\frac{3}{4}$ in. over the last seam line.

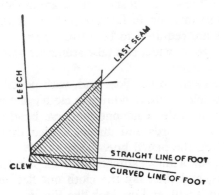

FIG. 8. Laying the first cloth of the foresail. The shaded portion represents the first cloth in position on the floor plan.

Now turn the cloth round (but not over), and with the newly cut edge overlapping the last seam line, again by $\frac{3}{4}$ in. (the cloth should fit exactly without waste), lay the second cloth, and cut off so that the edge overlaps the foot by $1\frac{1}{2}$ in. The second cloth overlaps the first by $\frac{1}{2}$ in., a sewing guide being drawn in pencil $\frac{1}{2}$ in. in from the edge of the first cloth, and along the corresponding edges of all subsequent cloths. The last seam line should also be drawn in pencil on the cloth.

Continue this process until the whole of the lower part of the sail plan is covered. Now, starting again from the clew, lay the cloth in exactly the same manner on the top part of the plan, overlapping the leech by $1\frac{1}{2}$ in., and the last seam by only $\frac{1}{4}$ in. In both cases, ensure that the cloth overlaps the luff by 4 in. (The amounts of overlap quoted apply to headsails with luff up to about 18 ft. For larger sails the amounts should be increased approximately in proportion to the area.)

The strike-up marks should be placed next. These are short pencil lines drawn across the real seams, at 1 ft. intervals. When the seams are sewn, the two halves of each mark must be made to match up, so that the seam will be sewn exactly as laid.

Complete the laying of the cloth by bending up the cut edges of the cloth on all three sides of the sail, and crease exactly along the curved lines of the luff, leech and foot. It is convenient to mark the crease with an intermittent pencil line. Then lift the cloths from the floor as follows:

Starting from the tack, take up the first cloth and place on the second. Then take up both the first and the second together and place on the third, and so on until you reach the clew. Now start again at the peak in the same manner until you again reach the clew, when you will have two piles of cloth ready for machining, and in the right order.

Starting on the lower half of the sail, sew the first and second cloths together, overlapping exactly as they were on the floor, first with one line of stitching $\frac{1}{8}$ in. in from the edge of the top cloth and then, after turning the cloth over, with a second similar line of stitching $\frac{1}{8}$ in. in from the edge of the other cloth. Remember to make the two halves of the strike-up marks match together as you sew. Ensure also that the bulk of the sail is to the left of the needle and the cloth just being added to the right, as otherwise, towards the end, the sail might not be able to go through the machine.

Next complete the false seams in the first two cloths.

Bend these down, all the same way throughout the sail, and sew down with two lines of stitching, one each side of the seam, so that the false seam looks exactly the same as the real seams. Proceed to add the cloths to the sail in this way until the clew is reached, then start again at the peak. Having completed the two halves of the sail, sew them together up the last seam in the same way, but turning in the edges ($\frac{1}{4}$ in. has been allowed for the turn in) making sure that the corresponding seams of the two halves meet exactly along the last seam.

Operation 6   Fitting the patches and tablings. Lay the sail out on the floor, the same way up as laid on the plan. The pencilled creases along each side of the sail will now have discrepancies owing to slight inaccuracies in seaming, so new creased lines should be drawn to allow for these, ensuring that these new lines form smooth curves.

The patches are cut out next, the peak and tack each having one under and one top patch, the clew having two under and one top patch (the purpose of the patches is merely to give the corners of the sail adequate strength).

The shapes of the patches should be as in Fig. 9, the peak and tack patches being 10 in. and 8 in. long respectively, and each arm of the clew patch 18 in. long (for larger sails, scale these sizes up in proportion to the area). The patches fit exactly on the pencilled creases of two sides of the sail, the remaining sides of the patches being drawn in on the sail in pencil. It is essential that the warp and weft of patches match exactly those of the sail.

For tack and peak, 1 in. inside these lines just drawn, draw similar lines exactly parallel, these last, with the creased pencilled lines, giving the shape of the under patches. For the clew, the two under patches are round and much smaller. Cut out the under patches exactly to these shapes, and sew on to the sail along the inner lines, just drawn, leaving the sides of the patches along the

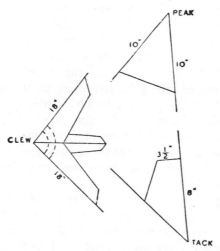

FIG. 9. Patches for the three corners of the foresail. The measurements shown are for an average sail of 50 sq. ft.

edges of the sail unsewn. In the case of the clew, the two under patches are put on together in the same manner (the edges of the under patches are not turned under).

Before sewing the top patches on, it is necessary to make and sew the tablings, (Fig. 10). On the leech and foot, an ordinary hem is made, finishing $\frac{3}{4}$ in. wide, $\frac{3}{4}$ in. being turned in, so that the tabling finishes three layers thick. This is sewn down with two rows of stitching, one each side of the hem or tabling. On the luff, the tabling is cut and turned, owing to the fact that the warp of the cloth meets the luff at an angle, it being

FIG. 10.   Elevation view of cut and resewn tabling.

most necessary that the warp of the tabling should lie in the same direction as that of the sail, as otherwise creases would appear (if the luff tabling is formed merely by turning in, as on the other two sides, the weave of the tabling does not match the sail at all). To cut and turn the tabling, for which 4 in. has been allowed, cut off a strip 3½ in. wide, leaving ½ in. outside the creases.

Bend upwards the ½ in. remaining on the sail outside the pencilled crease, and on the tabling which has just been cut off, bend ½ in. of each side downwards and in (leaving the tabling 2½ in. wide). Now move the tabling on to the edge of the sail (see Fig. 11A for end-on view) and move up the sail about 2 in. so that the seams across the tabling do not lie over the seams in the sail.

Although the tabling finishes in this position, it is necessary to have the seam along the edge of the luff to lie flat over the wire, and so — with the luff on your right, and the remainder of the sail on your left, hold the tabling and sail together with your left hand (the body of the sail remaining under your hand), and lift up. With your right hand, draw the sail to your right under the tabling. When it is clear of the tabling, place on the floor, and you have the position for sewing the line of stitching along the edge of the luff (Fig. 11B). Place this line of stitching as close to the edge of the tabling as possible.

Having completed this seam, bend the tabling back into its original position (Fig. 11A) and sew down with the second line of stitching along the other edge, not forgetting to place a string inside the tabling, before sewing up, with which to draw the luff wire through.

To complete operation 6, the outer patches are fitted (Fig. 9). These are cut out exactly the same size as the under patches, but with the extra 1 in. on the inboard sides, and also an additional $\frac{1}{2}$ in. is left all the way round. This $\frac{1}{2}$ in. is turned down and under. In the case of the clew, the patch is made up in two halves, seamed together, the seam lying along the last seam (the two halves of the patch are cut out in such a way as to ensure that the weave of the patch corresponds exactly with that in the sail) and is sewn down along the inboard sides with the machine, and is tacked in position by hand along the leech and foot, the tacking stitches being very short on the patch side of

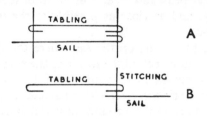

FIG. 11. Method of tabling.

the sail and long on the other side. The rope will cover the long part of the stitch, avoiding the necessity of removing the tacking.

The sewing on of the rope will, at the same time, complete the sewing of the patch (it is undesirable to sew the leech and foot sides with the machine as, especially in larger sails, the stitching would make the canvas stiffer and more difficult to rope). The tack and peak top patches are sewn by machine on the leech and foot sides, and the inboard sides excluding the tabling. They are then sewn by hand across the tabling (put something inside the tabling first, to make sure that it is kept open), and round seamed, or oversewn, along the luff. The sail is now ready for finishing.

Operation 7   Finishing. First make up the luff wire to the exact length of the luff required with a heart-shaped thimble spliced in at each end (for information on wire splicing see Chapter 3).

Parcel the luff wire along the whole length with strips of any lightweight material, such as cotton from old sheets, and over the parcelling, hitch the wire with marline hitches 1½ in. apart, using hand thread. Draw the wire into the luff tabling. Next sew two eyelets (small size) through the tabling at peak and tack, ½ in. in from foot and leech respectively, and as close as possible to the wire; in the following manner:

Place the brass ring on the sail where the eyelet is required to be, draw round the inside of the ring with pencil and make a round hole in the cloth half the internal diameter of the ring in size; with palm and needle, sew the ring to the sail round and round the metal of the ring, each stitch lying as close as possible to, and the same as, the last. The result is a sewn eyelet, which is much stronger than an ordinary brass one. Although the eyelet is satisfactory as it is, it is desirable to punch a brass turnover into the eyelet (when in position, the turnover looks like a round thimble), though of course a special punch and die is required.

The foot of the sail is roped towards the tack from 3 in. beyond the end of the tack patch, and this is done as follows:

First make the end of the rope (which should preferably be Italian hemp) into a tail (see Chapter 3).

Next take the turns out of the rope so that it is in a completely relaxed state, stretch tight and mark on it a straight line in blue pencil, or something similar. Take a chair without arms, and place it so that there is a heavy table or other fixed object a few feet away on the right hand side of the chair. Attach a sail hook (this can be bought for about 6d.) to a piece of line which is tied to the leg of the table. Now sit, and place the foot of the sail in your lap with the patch uppermost and the luff wire on your right, and the tabling towards the body. Insert the sail hook in the sewn eyelet at the tack and draw the hook line tight. Lift up the foot of the sail, so that it is vertical, and place the rope along the edge, on the near side, the point of the tail being 3 in. to the left of the end of the patch, and the line marked on the rope along the edge of the tabling.

Now with needle and palm, and hand thread (waxed), oversew the point of the rope on to the edge of the tabling for ½ in. and then continue as follows:

Insert the needle through the rope (pointing away from you) so that it goes cleanly between the strands, leaving two strands below and one above the needle (care must be taken that the needle does not catch any of the fibres of the strands, and to help in this it is desirable that the needle should not be too sharp). Keeping the rope carefully in position, press the needle through the sail and pull the thread tight to the left (for large sails, it is desirable to obtain extra pull by winding the thread a few times round a wooden handle, and then twisting the handle). Continue roping until you reach the sewn eyelet, then bend the rope round the eyelet, as close as possible to the eyelet (i.e. going between the eyelet and the wire), sew down to the sail securely, and cut the rope clean off just above the eyelet.

Next stretch the luff wire tight between two points at about chest height. At each end, seize the sewn eyelet to the thimble in the wire with marline, adjusting the seizing so that the luff of the sail is drawn out to its fully stretched measurement. Then at 2 ft. intervals along the luff, place

E

a seizing round the wire to stop the cloth moving along the wire. Fix the luff of the sail to the luff wire with a sticking stitch the whole length. This stitch is very simple and is done, as mentioned earlier, by pressing the needle through the tabling, away from you, as close to the wire as possible, moving along a little and coming straight back again, moving along again, and again sewing through the cloth close to the wire, and so on. In order to make this stitch as neat as possible, insert the needle at an angle in the direction of progress, nearly all the forward movement being then carried out in the cloth, and only very small stitches showing on each side.

In cases where maximum area is required, it is usual to set the tack wire eye into the sail, which is done in the following manner:

Measure the length of the actual eye of the wire, and make a pencil mark on the outside edge of the luff tabling this distance from the tack end. Split with a knife the edge of the tabling as far as the mark, so that when the wire is placed in position, the outside half of the wire loop is visible, and the inside half is between the sail and the tabling.

Next draw a pencil line on the tabling over the inside edge of the inner half of the wire loop. Remove the wire and cut away the cloth along this pencil line, so that when the wire is replaced the whole of the interior of the wire loop is visible, but the inner half of the actual wire is not.

Tack the loop in place with a few stitches, and then oversew with hand thread the inner half of the wire loop, starting at the splice end, and keeping the stitches as close together as possible. As soon as the edge of the canvas on the outside of the loop is reached, sew the foot rope, as per normal roping instructions, also to this point.

Spread out the three strands of rope so that they lie over the wire evenly, and continue with the needle and thread, but instead of sewing the wire to the sail the thread will be binding the rope to the wire. After a very short distance, shave the rope with a knife so that it roughly comes to a point at the upper end of the outside half of the loop. Bind this to the wire with the turns of the thread lying not too close together, and serve over the external part of the loop with marline. Lastly knock in the thimble with a mallet, fidding out the loop if necessary.

The eye of the wire is also sometimes set in at the head, but less frequently, especially as it is desirable to have the wire a little longer than the sail, so that if the sail should at any time overstretch, the canvas can be drawn a little tighter along the wire (Fig. 12).

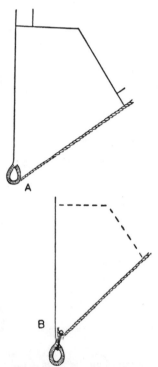

FIG. 12. Tack thimble of a foresail (A) set in the sail for maximum area, and (B) set below the sail.

Finish the clew by roping from a point on the leech a few inches above the end of the clew liner top, round the clew and finishing at a point again a few inches beyond the other extremity of the clew liner; having fitted either a large sewn eyelet or two small sewn eyelets, to which is fitted a grommet and round brass thimble. In larger sails, additional smaller sewn eyelets are fitted further inboard and lashed to the main eyelets for additional strength.

Finally, clean the sail, particularly at the points of working, with French chalk or bread.

Genoas

This last section deals with the special procedure to be followed in the making of Genoas, where this is different

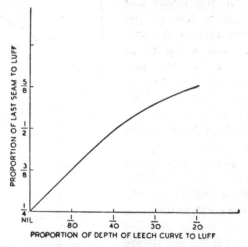

Fig. 13. Graph for calculating the depth of the leech curve on the floor plan for a Genoa, e.g. if the last seam is half the length of the luff, the depth of the curve would be one-fortieth of the length of the luff. The greatest depth of leech hollow occurs one-quarter of the way down from the head.

from the ordinary foresails which, for convenience, we have taken to be all headsails where the last seam is one quarter, or less, of the luff.

The two main differences are the hollowing of the leech and the slight cross cutting of the leech and foot. For our ordinary foresails, the leech is straight, but as the last seam lengthens, the leech is progressively more deeply hollowed. The hollow is a regular curve whose depth may be calculated from the graph (Fig. 13). Suppose the genoa has luff 24 ft. and last seam 16 ft., then the proportion of last seam to luff will be ·6667. Mark this point on the vertical scale, follow the horizontal line until it cuts the curve. At this point drop vertically downwards to the horizontal scale, which gives the proportion of depth of hollow to luff as one-twentieth (=14½ in.).

Having marked in the hollow leech curve, mark a point one-sixth of the way down the leech, and draw a line at right angles to the *curved* line of the leech. This should be produced both ways so that the line is about the length of the foot. Having marked on the last seam the point where the right hand edge of the first cloth will lie, draw through this point a line parallel to the one just drawn. Then, also through the point, draw another line striking the foot and making to the last seam the same angle as the first. These two lines mark the edges of the first two cloths to be laid, and the laying of the remainder should proceed in exactly the same way as for ordinary foresails. (The last seam should be drawn in as before, bisecting the angle between the *straight* lines of leech and foot. The curves given to the foot should not increase with the length of foot, and should be about the same in depth as for ordinary foresails.)

Stretch luffs for headsails

The object is to produce a full sail for sailing off the wind which yet can be flattened for windward work. This can be done either by using a special stretch bolt rope to contract the luff of the sail when relaxed, being hauled taut for flattening the sail by means of a mast winch, a tack purchase or by a Cunningham hole fitted as per the mainsail or operating so that the luff of the sail slides on the luff wire. (See Page 81).

CHAPTER 5

THE BERMUDIAN MAINSAIL

THE Bermudian mainsail became popular between the wars as it proved to be much more efficient for windward work than the original gaff sail. In the early days of yachting when hull design was less advanced and the hulls themselves had less windward ability, the gaff mainsail was ideal, giving maximum efficiency off the wind and having a shorter mast more easily stayed; and added to this the stowing of the topsail formed a very convenient method of reefing. But now, with the emphasis more and more on sailing to windward, nearly all modern yachts and dinghies set Bermudian sails.

As every sailor, and particularly perhaps the racing man, appreciates, the shape of the curve in which the sail sets is of vital importance. In principle the sail should be so shaped that, with the hull sailing at maximum advantage on the wind, the whole sail will be drawing and no part of it empty of wind; but at the same time it should have the maximum flow or belly that this requirement allows. Then, if the sail is perfect, the curve of the sail will appear fair and smooth from whatever point on luff, leech or foot the eye is placed.

The fullness of the sail is produced by cutting the luff and foot as convex curves and fitting these to straight spars. The depth and shape of the curves control the fullness, though generally speaking it is mainly the depth only that is variable, the position of maximum depth on any given curve usually being one third of the distance from the tack along luff or foot.

Having determined the shape the sail is to be cut, it is necessary to lay the cloths in such a way as to ensure that it will remain the same shape in whatever weather it is set. The yarns of which the cloth is woven will themselves stretch little, but if the material is pulled on the cross, or diagonally, the stretch will be considerable, additional

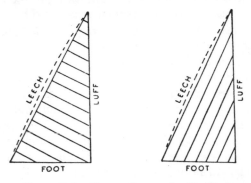

FIG. 14. Cuts of the Bermudian mainsail. Horizontal cut and vertical cut.

length being gained at the expense of area lost elsewhere. So, as the sail is triangular, at least one side of the sail must be cut on the cross. The tack being almost right-angular, this one side would be the leech. Practical considerations, such as the fact that the leech is not fitted to a spar, prevent the sail being cut in this way. When everything is taken into consideration, it is found that the best way is to cut both the luff and foot on the cross, both these being supported by spars and bolt ropes, and leaving the leech to be unsupported satisfactorily (Fig. 14). And to gain area the leech is cut as a convex curve, the additional cloth being held in place by the battens.

Where the sides are cut on the cross, they must be prevented from stretching by the fitting of a wire or rope. Thus a Bermudian mainsail is roped along luff and foot, the leech remaining unsupported except by a tabling of self material, this somewhat equivalent to the hem of a garment. These provisions will ensure that the sail remains the correct shape in use, but owing to the fact that the actual yarns stretch a certain amount, the whole sail must be made smaller than the required size by a predetermined amount, varying according to the type and quality of the cloth (see Chapter 2).

To ensure that the flow of the sail is exactly as required when the stretching is complete, it is necessary to be very careful as to how the rope is fitted to the luff and foot, and the tabling to the leech. It is highly desirable to use the best quality rope (Italian hemp is usually chosen), partly as the yarns stretch less and partly because the rope is laid up tighter. All normal ropes stretch in two ways, first in the yarns of which the rope is made, and second in the fact that the lay can be tightened by pulling the rope, giving additional strength. It has been found by experiment exactly how much a particular sailcloth will stretch, and equally the stretch of any given rope can be determined. The easiest way to do this is to stretch the rope tightly between two uprights about 3 ft. from the floor and suspend a weight from the middle of it. This will gradually stretch the rope until it touches the floor. The rope should then be tightened and the procedure repeated until the weight no longer drops.

Having ascertained the stretched length of the rope, this has to be sewn to the sail in such a way that when the sailcloth is fully stretched, the rope attached to it is also. As the rope stretches considerably more than the sailcloth, allowance for this has to be made in the actual stitching of the rope to the cloth, by taking in with each stitch a little extra cloth. This amount can be calculated mathematically, but of course, in normal sailmaking the exact method of making each stitch, so that the required result is achieved, is found by experience, and is given in the second half of this chapter.

Though the leech tabling can quite satisfactorily be made in the form of an ordinary hem by turning in the edge of the cloth twice, the best sails show a more specialised tabling method. The tabling is first cut from the sail and then resewn, making allowance for the fact that the tabling, being thicker, will stretch a little less than the sailcloth, and for the fact that as the leech is convex curved, the majority of it is cut very slightly on the cross.

To give the sail adequate strength, each corner must be substantially reinforced, particularly to take the strain of halyard, clew outhaul, etc. This is done by fitting several patches which become more numerous and more comprehensive as the sail gets larger. The eyelets at the tack and clew are sewn in, and in the larger sails are attached to one or more smaller eyelets sewn close to the main eyelets.

The tack of a mainsail has to take rather more strain than other parts, and consequently tends to stretch more, allowance for which is made by broad-seaming. This involves making the overlap of the cloths in the vicinity of the tack widen slightly as they approach the tack. The seams then look wider than normal, and the distance between them is less. Initially this induces additional flow into the sail, but when stretching is complete this will disappear. Where the warp or weft of the cloth strikes either the luff or the foot at a greater angle than the other, the seams here should tend to be broader to allow for the fact that the cloth, being cut here more on the cross, will tend to stretch more.

Broad-seaming at the tack of mainsails is a most important matter. If it is not done the set of the sail will almost certainly be unsatisfactory, and we think it safe to say that broad-seams will be found in all good mainsails, mentioning in passing that it is not entirely safe to assume that a sail which has uniform width of seam is not broad-seamed, as sails have been made where the surplus cloth has been removed from the broad-seam in order to keep the seam the same width (we think that possibly the purpose of this has been to keep sailmaking employees guessing in case they should desire to gather enough information to enable them to start in business on their own).

Reefing and reef points should be considered with care as much depends on their efficiency. One has heard a saying 'by thy reefs shall ye be known', suggesting, we feel, disapproval of the inefficient way in which sails are sometimes reefed. The secret of a good reef is to ensure that the foot is pulled out tight (taking care to avoid over-stretching, as there will not be the restraining influence of the bolt rope), before the points are tied down. This, coupled with the fact that the row of points should be fitted slightly below the line joining the two cringles, ensures that most of the strain is taken by the cringles and not by the reef points.

In general the reef points are arranged so that when reefed some of the fullness is removed from the sail, and an interesting variation from the normal reef is that often fitted to racing sails where the points run a few inches only from the foot, enabling the sail to be flattened without diminishing in size.

Roller reefing is popular owing to the ease with which it enables a reef to be taken, but for set of sail the resulting reef cannot really be compared with a tied reef. If the boom is exactly the right shape (oval, with the ends smaller and round, seems to be best), the sail can be maintained in a fairly good shape for, say, four rolls, but it would appear impossible to prevent the boom dropping (more and more the greater the number of rolls). The reason for this is mainly that it is scarcely possible to keep the foot stretched out tight as the sail is rolled.

Owing to the fact that the reefing gear is more bulky than the normal tack fitting, the tack of the sail will have to be fitted a few inches further away from the mast. This may be allowed for by fitting the mast track to a batten to keep the track in line with the tack — this, though efficient, tends to be ugly. Or a short batten for the lower few feet of the luff can be fitted to lead the sail out to clear the reefing gear. In this case the sail must be made to fit, and when it is reefed the set of the sail tends to be less efficient. Or, again, perhaps the simplest method, the mast track stops two or three feet above the boom, and the luff of the sail is shaped to run straight from this point to the tack and is kept in position by lacing.

The last consideration is the leech line, which consists of a light line fastened below the headboard and running down the leech inside the tabling, emerging through a small eyelet just above the top reef. Its purpose is to prevent the leech flapping should this tendency arise. It is usually operated from the clew in such a way as it is impossible to get at when under way, being often therefore considered as a mere nuisance. This seems a pity, as we have found it a first class piece of equipment if the line is led round the clew and along the boom to the tack, and is operated while standing at the mast. If there should be no tendency to flap, care should be taken to see that the leech line is left slack.

* * * * *

The Bermudian mainsail is made in six operations, as follows:

Tools required

Needles, wax, chalk, palm, string and tape, sail hook, mallet and hammer, sharp knife.

Operation 1   A plan of the sail is first drawn on the floor in chalk, the three sides being represented by straight lines the exact lengths of the sides of the sail before stretching. The difference between the stretched and unstretched lengths may be calculated as follows: On luff and foot, where the cloth is cut at an angle to the warp and weft, the difference would be 1 ft. in 20 ft. of stretched size, and on the leech, cut at right-angles to warp and weft 6 in. in 20 ft. stretched size.

Draw the luff in first on the right hand side of the floor, with the foot nearest to you, and place the headboard in position (Fig. 15), drawing round it with chalk (headboards are either of wood or aluminium, and are usually the shape of an isosceles triangle, the short sides lying along the luff and across the top of the sail). The leech and foot are then drawn in by a makeshift compass of chalk and string. Fixing the chalk to the string, and making the string the exact length of the foot, and with centre the base of the luff, draw an arc covering the position of the clew; again, making the string the exact length of the leech, and with centre at the left hand, or outer, corner of the headboard, draw a second arc to cut the first. The clew then lies at the point of intersection and is joined by straight lines to the centres used.

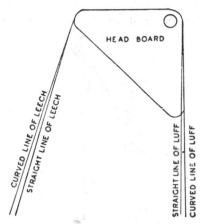

FIG. 15. Position of the headboard on the floor plan of the Bermudian mainsail.

All three sides of the sail have convex curves (Fig. 16), which are drawn on the plan as follows — Luff: measure along the luff from the tack one third of the length of the luff, and at the point found measure outwards 1 in. for every 5 ft. of the length of the luff on the plan (i.e. for a luff of 20 ft. measure outwards 4 in.). Foot: from the tack, measure one third the length of the foot, and at this point measure downward an amount equivalent to 1 in. in every 3 ft. 6 in. of the foot. Leech: at a point half-way along the leech, measure outwards an amount equivalent to 1 ft. in 25 ft. Now join the two ends of each side by smooth curves passing through the points found, the maximum depths of the curves being at these points (Fig. 16). (A tape-measure or something similar should be used to make the curve.

This is adjusted until the curve is approved, and then the curve is drawn in in chalk). The accuracy of the curves can be checked by placing the eye at one end near the ground and looking along the curve, when any irregularities will immediately be apparent.

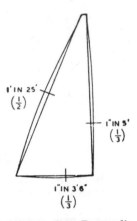

FIG. 16. Floor plan of the Bermudian mainsail. The depths of the curve are as shown, and the fractions in brackets indicate the proportion of the distance the maximum depths lie from the ends of the curves, e.g. the maximum depth of the luff curve is one-third the distance from the tack to the peak.

These measurements can be considered average for an average mainsail, but they may be varied to meet special requirements. If the sail is for a fast racing type boat which can point really well, the curves on the luff and foot may be lessened slightly; and if the yacht is a cruiser where sailing off the wind is more important, then the curves may be increased a little. And again, should the foot be exceptionally long, the curve here should be less until, if the foot is the same length as the luff, the curves on both would be equal.

The floor plan is finished by drawing in the tack seam, represented by a line joining the tack to the leech, cutting the latter at right-angles.

Operation 2   False seaming the cloth. For larger mainsails, 18 in. cloths are usual and satisfactory, requiring, in 36 in. cloth, one false seam; though 12 in. and even 9 in. cloths may be desired for best results (these latter naturally make for more expense owing to the additional cloth needed, and the time in sewing a larger number of seams). 12 in. cloths are most suitable for small sails, and perhaps 9 in. for very small ones. The false seams are made as described in Chapter 3, by drawing a line down the cloth to represent the seam, folding the cloth along this line, with the line outwards. In the case of smaller sails, of up to say 150 sq. ft. sew the two parts of the cloth together exactly $\frac{1}{2}$ in. in from the crease and pencil line, using a white thread (which will not show when the seam is finished). For larger sails, the width of the seam should be increased proportionately. The false seam will be finished at a later stage, but the cloth is now ready for laying on the plan. All the cloth should be false-seamed before proceeding with the next operation.

Operation 3   Laying the cloth (the measurements given here will apply to small sails up to about 150 sq. ft. but they should be increased in proportion for larger sails, which automatically require wider seams, larger tablings, etc.). Unroll a length of the cloth and lay with lower edge along the tack seam line, with false seams uppermost, so that the end overlaps the curved line of the leech by $2\frac{1}{2}$ in. Stretch the cloth out as tight as you reasonably can, and fix to the floor either with pins or weights. Now cut the cloth from the roll so that the end overlaps the curved line of the luff by 5 in. (Fig. 17).

Before laying the next cloth it is necessary to draw a sewing guide in pencil along the upper edge of the first cloth, starting at the leech end, $\frac{1}{2}$ in. in from the selvedged edge, and increasing to $\frac{3}{4}$ in. from the edge at the luff end. This marks a broad seam on which a general note follows

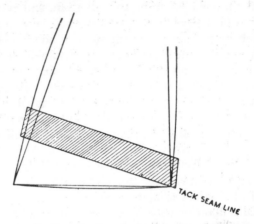

FIG. 17. Laying the first cloth of the Bermudian main-sail. The shaded portion represents the first cloth.

shortly. Now lay the second cloth, starting at the luff end, so that its edge lies along the sewing guide just drawn, again with the sewing guide and false seam uppermost, maintaining the 5 in. overlap at the luff and cutting off so that the leech overlap is again $2\frac{1}{2}$ in. It will be noted that in order to keep the false seams uppermost, the cloth must not be turned over; it is, in fact, turned round so that the cut removing the first cloth from the main length fits exactly along the luff to form the beginning of the second cloth.

Proceed similarly at the leech and it will be found that there should be no waste of cloth at all.

Draw a sewing guide on the second cloth, broad-seaming if necessary, but otherwise maintaining the seam parallel at ½ in. (see paragraph on broad-seaming below),

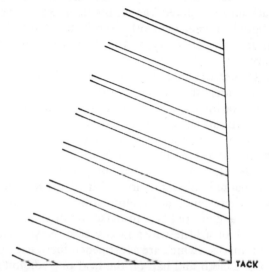

FIG. 18. The appearance of broad seams at the tack of a Bermudian mainsail.

and proceed laying the cloths in the same way until the peak is reached.

Now start laying the cloths below the tack seam line, drawing the sewing guide first (broad seamed) and placing the cloth under the first cloth laid, so that the edge of the latter lies along the sewing guide. Continue laying the cloths until the whole plan is covered.

Note on broad-seaming (Fig. 18). The broad-seam is in-

F

corporated to allow for additional stretch in the tack, and is placed only in the vicinity of the tack, covering say 3 to 4 seams. When laying the cloth, and starting from the leech, the seam should be parallel for half the length and then should widen gradually until, at the tack, it is about twice as wide. This involves laying the straight edge of the cloth on to a curved line on the floor, which theoretically should prevent the cloth from being able to lay flat, but in fact the elasticity of the cloth itself avoids this difficulty.

The greater the angle at which the cloth strikes luff or foot, the wider should the broad seam be made. One should not be mislead, however, into supposing that in the average mainsail the angles at foot and luff are very different, as in a mainsail of aspect ratio 2 to 1, the warp strikes the luff at the same angle as the weft does the foot. Thus only very short or very long footed sails should show a marked difference in width of broad-seam. As, however, there tends to be more strain on the foot than the luff, it is good practice to make the broad seams that strike the foot a little wider in any case. Next, place the strike-up marks, (which are short pencil lines, each placed half on one cloth and half on the next one adjoining, the two halves being matched up in sewing the cloths together) in pencil at 1 ft. intervals across every real seam, the two halves of each having to be matched up when sewing the seam, and to complete the laying of the cloth bend up the cut edges on all three sides of the sail and crease exactly along the curved lines of the luff, leech and foot, marking the creases with an intermittent pencil line. The cloths should now be lifted ready for sewing as follows: Lift the top cloth without turning it over or round, and place on the cloth immediately below. Lift these two cloths and place on the third cloth, and so on until all the cloths are in one pile.

Operation 4 Sewing the cloths. Take the cloth at the top of the pile, and the next, and place together exactly as they were on the plan. Sew along the edge of the upper cloth, about ⅛ in. in from the edge, ensuring that the strike-up marks match up, and that the edge of the cloth stays on the sewing guide. Now turn the cloth over and sew a second line of stitching ⅛ in. in from the edge of the other cloth, to complete the seam. Turn the cloth back again, and sew down the false seams in the first two cloths, with two lines of stitching to each seam, each ⅛ in. in from the edge of the seam, arranging that all the false seams should be flattened with the cloth the same way, either upwards or downwards, so that the widths of the cloths do not vary. Join each succeeding cloth to the sail in the same way, making sure that the bulk of the sail is always to the left of the machine to avoid difficulty in passing it between the needle and the main upright.

Operation 5 Rubbing down to make the sail ready for finishing. Lay the sail on the floor the same way up as before and, on all three sides, turn up the edges along the original pencilled creases and crease down sharply, allowing for the discrepancies which will have appeared after machining and ensuring that the crease shows a really smooth curve, as this is the final edge of the sail. On the luff and foot draw a line parallel to this crease and ¾ in. outside it; the cloth on the outside of this will be cut off and sewn on again to form the tabling. Before cutting, however, the tabling guide lines should be drawn — these being two lines, 2½ in. apart in the case of the luff and 2 in. for the foot, placed centrally (Fig. 19) — and the patches cut out ready for fitting.

The function of the patches (and tablings) is merely to strengthen the sail at the points of strain, and their shapes are as shown in Fig. 20. In smaller sails of up to say 20 ft. luff, there are in each case one top and two under patches, the sizes being shown as in Fig. 20, scaling up proportionately for larger sails. Draw out the patches on a spare piece of sailcloth. Cut out the top patches, leaving ½ in. all round for turning in. Then cut out the under patches in the same way, but along the pencil lines, without leaving

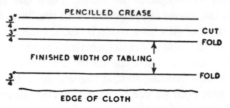

FIG. 19. Diagram representing the tabling before being cut from the sail.

any margin for turning in. Sew the under patches on with a line of stitching ½ in. from the edge of the patch along the inboard sides only, leaving the luff, leech and foot sides unsewn, as these will be sewn automatically with the roping (one under patch is sewn in this way to the sail, and the other to the outer side of the top patch, to allow flexibility). Preserve the top patches, as the tablings are fitted next and under the top patches.

Starting with the leech, which cuts the cloths at right-angles, form the tabling by turning the cloth in twice, first by 1¼ in. and then again by 1¼ in. (this latter along the pencilled crease), and sew down with a line of stitching close to each side of the tabling, which finished 1¼ in. wide (the leech line should be placed in position before the

tabling is sewn down, as described in a note at the end).
On the other two sides, luff and foot, which cut the cloths
at an angle, the tablings must be cut and turned (were they
to be fitted similarly to the leech tabling the weave in the

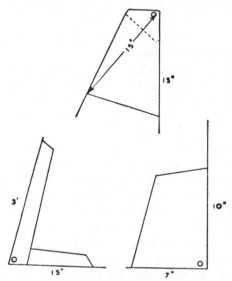

FIG. 20. Patches of the Bermudian sail. The measurements are for an average mainsail of 100 sq. ft.

tabling would not correspond to that in the sail, and
creases might result). Cut the tabling from the sail, on the
¾ in. outside the creased pencil line, and without turning
the tabling over or round, place it on the edge of the sail,
with the edges turned down and inwards. Move the tabling
along the sail about 3 in. to ensure that the seams in the
tabling do not correspond with those in the sail, this
merely to ensure ease of stitching and roping. Sew the
tablings down with two lines of stitching as in the case of

the leech.

Note on patches for larger sails. In general, the larger the sail the more numerous and complex should be the patches. The shapes remain roughly the same, but at the clew and tack a foot-liner is fitted in addition, and for large sails a strainer as well. Liner and strainer under patches may also be fitted, all the additional patches being left to the discretion of the sailmaker.

Fit next the top patches, turning down and inwards the spare $\frac{1}{2}$ in. left all round, and sewing to the sail with a line of stitching close to the edge all the way round each patch, except the luff and top edges of the peak patch, these sides requiring special treatment to allow the fitting of the headboard. This is placed between the sail and the top patch in such a way that the top and luff edges lie exactly on those of the sail; turn the cloth in and under itself, keeping it the same side of the headboard, so that the edge just overlaps the edge of the headboard, and when bent over will meet the cloth from the other side exactly in the middle. The top leading corner of the headboard contains the eye for the halyard shackle, and this should be uncovered by turning the cloth further inwards across the corner. Sew the headboard in position through the holes provided, very strongly, with hand thread, and complete with a normal hand stitch, by sewing together, across the edges of the headboard, the cloths overlapping each side, so that they are pulled tight and just meet.

Mark in the batten pockets next at equal intervals down the leech, smaller mainsails usually having three and larger sails four; in the latter case the two centre battens being longer than the top and lower ones. Ordinarily, the battens lie parallel to the cloths, but the lower one is often placed horizontal to allow maximum space for reefing.

Mark the batten pockets on the sail with pencil, making them $\frac{1}{2}$ in. wider and longer than the actual batten (this is important to ensure that the batten can be extracted when the sail is wet).

From the spare sailcloth, cut out the patches to shape, making sure that the weave of the patches corresponds exactly to that in the sail, to avoid setting up strains in the cloth, and, turning the edges down and inwards, sew to the sail with one line of stitching so that the patch fits exactly the plan of the pocket. On the leech end, an additional 1 in. of cloth should be left and then turned in double for strength. The stitching along the sides of the pocket is stopped $\frac{1}{2}$ in. short of the leech, to allow the batten to be inserted easily, and two sewn eyelets, as described later, are worked in the flap. On the sail, opposite these two eyelets, the centre of a short length of cotton line is sewn in such a way that the two whipped ends may be threaded through the holes in both the batten and pocket, and then tied with a reef knot.

If reef points are required, they may be fitted as follows: decide how deep to make the reef, and draw a pencil line on the sail representing the row of reef points, this following the line of the foot and being parallel to it (it is perhaps desirable to raise this line at the leech end by an inch or two in order to counteract the boom's tendency to drop when the sail is reefed, due to its proportionately greater length and weight as compared with the sail area and length of foot. At 1 ft. intervals along the line, sew a diamond patch cut from spare cloth with edges turned in, measuring for small sails $2\frac{1}{2}$ in. high by 2 in. wide, and again having the weave corresponding to that of the sail.

In the middle of each diamond, work a sewn eyelet. At

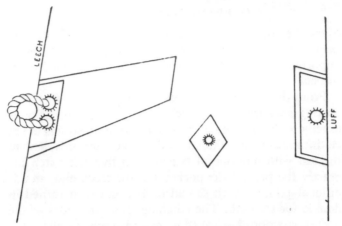

FIG. 21. Reef patches. At both luff and leech, the smaller patches shown are the under patches. The diamond patch is one out of the row across the sail. (Note that its point is on a line joining eyelet and cringle.)

each end of the line of points, fit an under and top patch (shaped as in Fig. 21), fitting these exactly as the corner patches, the under patch being under, and the top patch over, the tabling, in the case of the leech, and both being under the tabling at the luff. Here one large sewn eyelet should be worked, and at the leech, two small sewn eyelets, $1\frac{1}{2}$ in. apart, these latter to take a rope cringle, which is fitted after the sail has been roped. In order that the cringle and large eyelet should take most of the weight, they should be placed in line with the top points of the diamonds (Fig. 21).

Rather as people wonder how on earth yards move yachts about on land, it often seems a puzzle to know how the round thimble is held so tightly in the cringle. But, as usual, the answer is very simple, though doing the job requires some practice. Make the cringle smaller than the thimble, open it by knocking it down a fid, or large wooden spike, with a mallet until it is expanded to the correct size; then knock it suddenly off the fid and bang the thimble in before the rope has had time to contract. This must be done very quickly indeed, and it is a matter of experiment to expand the grommet the right amount.

To complete the reef, make up a reef tier in cotton line for each point, whipping both ends to finish approximately 2 ft. long. A tier is then placed through each eyelet so that it is the same length both sides; both parts are bent downwards and sewn together through the sail, immediately below the eyelet. It should be noted that the leech should be roped in way of each row of reef points, the rope either running up from the clew as a continuous length, or in the form of short lengths each with two tails, and each covering a row of reefs.

The leeches of most mainsails show a considerable convex curve which, though held in position by the battens, sometimes has a tendency to flap, especially in the wind, for which the cure is the leech line. This consists of a thin line spliced into the rope along the leech immediately below the headboard, passing into the tabling through a small eyelet, which is fitted before the tabling is sewn down, and leaving the tabling again through a similar eyelet placed just above the top reef. Thus a flap in the leech may be stopped by tautening the leech line.

The headboard is fitted next. Place between the sail and the head patch. The luff side has already been sewn up. Use the headboard, pushing this tight against the luff stitching, to show exactly where the stitching along the head is to come, sew by hand across the top of the sail in such a way that the two turned-in edges of the cloth will just meet across the top of the headboard. Push the headboard tightly into position in the corner just formed (it should fit the pencil lines previously drawn), and fix in position with two stitches. Using double thickness hand thread, twisted together, sew through each hole in the headboard, down one, up the next, down the following one and so on. On reaching the last hole, return in the same way, but with the stitch lying along the other side of the headboard, thus completing the stitch between each hole. Leave the halyard shackle hole uncovered by turning the cloth in and under each side. For convenience, the position of the sewing holes may be marked in pencil on the canvas by the use of a paper template made by a paper and pencil rubbing of the headboard. Also memorise the shape and details of the headboard before putting in the sail.

Operation 6   Roping and finishing. Eyelets should now be sewn into the tack and clew ½ in. in from each edge, in the following manner: place the brass ring of the eyelet on the sail in the correct position, and round the inside of the ring draw a circle in pencil half the internal diameter of the ring. With needle and palm, sew the ring to the sail, round the metal of the ring, each stitch lying as close as possible to, and the same size as the last. The eyelet is now satisfactory as it stands, except, as in the case of these two, where shackles will wear the thread. To avoid this, the eyelet is finished by punching a round brass thimble into the eyelet with a special punch and die. If slides are to be used on luff and foot, similar though smaller eyelets are placed ½ in. in from the edge, 15 in. apart along the luff, and 9 in. along the foot (these intervals scaling up for larger sails).

Roping completes the sail, and is a very important part of sailmaking, controlling, as it does, to a large extent, the satisfactory set of the sail. Start by making a tail at the end of the rope, by unlaying the strands, shaving with a knife, waxing, and laying up, as more fully described in Chapter 3. Next take the turns out of the rope, so that it is in a completely relaxed state, and mark a guide line on it with suitable chalk (blue) the whole way along the rope (to make it possible to see that the rope remains in its relaxed state).

Start roping at a point 3 in. above the top of the clew liner (the long patch running up the leech from the clew). Remembering that the rope is always fitted on the port side of the sail, this to assist in handling the sail in the dark — position the sail for roping as described in Chapter 3, sewing first the point of the tail and proceeding to the clew, keeping the guide line exactly along the edge of the sail.

As the rope stretches more than the sailcloth it is necessary to take in extra cloth with each stitch. By practice the right amount can be taken without difficulty, but otherwise it is desirable to fix the rope to the sail at 12 in. intervals, by first stretching the rope, the end attached to a fixed object, as tight as possible; laying the edge of the sail (tight but unstretched) along it, marking both rope and sail at 12 in. intervals; and then attaching the rope to the sail with temporary lashings (through the lay of the rope) at each mark, so that all the marks correspond. When the rope is relaxed, it will be seen that, for every foot of rope there is additional sail to be taken up — and this is taken up at each stitch, after the needle has entered between the lays of rope, by moving the point of the needle a little to the right before pressing it through the canvas.

Fitting head and clew for luff and foot groove

The headboard is fitted in the same way except that the luff edge of the headboard is 1 in. (or a little more for big sails) away from the luff of the sail. This 1 in. of cloth is stiffened before roping by several rows of stitching.

Unlike the normal fitting, the luff rope and the rope tail running over the top of the headboard and finishing a short way down the leech, are quite separate. Before the headboard is fitted in between the layers of cloth, the tail rope is fitted to the headboard so that it comes up the leech, along the top of the headboard (outside the canvas as before), and then, going through the canvas, down the leading edge of the headboard, being here securely tied to the headboard. The headboard is then sewn to the canvas as before.

The luff rope now ends exactly level with the top of the headboard. Serve the end of the rope for a length of 1½ in. and then sew to the canvas as before, using double stitch, and making sure that at the top it is sewn very securely.

The foot rope is fitted at the clew in exactly the same way as the luff rope at the headboard. Care should be taken, however, that the turnover at the clew is raised slightly, so that there is room for the groove between the foot rope and the turnover. Instead of the foot rope going round the clew and up the leech, it is separate as at the head. The bottom 2 or 3 in. of the leech rope is unlayed and plaited, so that it is soft and will lie flat; it is then curved round under the clew turnover and sewn to the canvas, finishing in a point.

Fitting sail number and insignia

Both numbers and insignia should be drawn in pencil on the sail both sides, making sure that the number and insignia one side are above and clear of those the other side of the sail, and that they are clear of batten pockets.

Where a cross-stitch machine is used, the numbers and insignia may be cut out exactly to shape, and sewn on flat, the outer end of the stitch just going over the edge of the cloth. Where a straight stitch is used, allowance for turning in should be made when cutting out.

It is most necessary, in fitting each number, to allow for shrinkage of the cloth from which the numbers are cut, by sewing on each number slightly slack. If they are sewn without any slack, and then the number shrinks, it may wrinkle the sail.

Fully battened mainsail to allow of increasing the area by a much deeper leech round.

This sail is made exactly as an ordinary Bermudian mainsail, with the exception that for best results the sail-cloth should lie at right angles to the actual curve of the leech, producing a radial effect. The full length batten pockets should lie over the seams, using batten stops on the inner end so that the battens are kept clear of the luff, and fitting tyers on the outer end of the batten pocket, rather than slots, so that the tension of each batten can be individually adjusted.

Making a sail with Cunningham hole

The Cunningham hole itself is a sewn eyelet (ref. Page 32) fitted in the luff tabling 6 to 9 inches up from the tack at a distance of 3/8ths of an inch between the bolt rope and the edge of the sewn eyelet stitching. In positioning the Cunningham hole it is necessary first to make sure that in operation it will not interfere with the luff groove in the mast.

For operation of the Cunningham hole a special stretch bolt rope (usually nylon) is required in place of the ordinary bolt rope. It is fitted in exactly the same way, except that it is essential to seize the rope strongly to the sail at 12 inches intervals up the luff through the rope and the sail in order to make sure that when the luff is stretched both cloth and rope are stretched together, and return together afterwards.

CHAPTER 6

THE GAFF MAINSAIL;
ALSO GUNTER LUGSAILS

THE gaff mainsail is more often cut vertically (Fig. 22), in order to give the leech maximum strength. The strain on the leech is greater than in the case of the Bermudian sail as the boom is usually heavier, and if the gaff is peaked too high, all the boom's weight is on the leech.

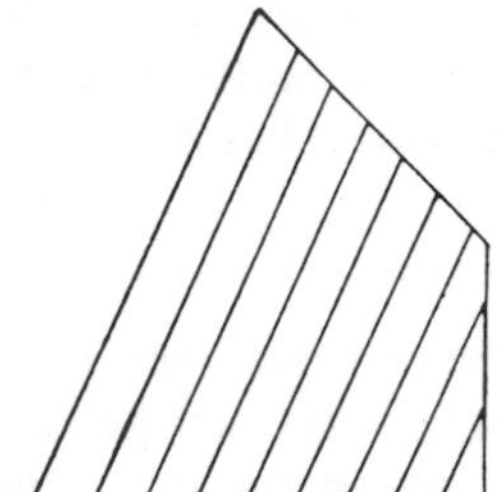

Most of the general remarks on the Bermudian mainsail apply also to the gaff sail. The cut is the major difference, but there are also some lesser ones. For instance, the leech is cut nearly straight rather than on a deeper convex curve, as the latter would give only a negligible increase in area; leech-lines and battens are thus unnecessary. Again, as gaff-rigged vessels are generally less efficient to windward, it is usual to make the sail a little fuller; and as the vessels are often more solidly built, a heavier cloth is chosen, requiring stronger bolt ropes, thread, etc.

FIG. 22. Cut of a gaff mainsail, verticle cut. Gaff mainsails are also cut horizontally with cloths at right angles to leech, but this is not recommended.

Owing to larger expanse of sail bounded by shorter sides, there is considerable tendency for the head and foot to over-stretch, as at the tack of the Bermudian sail. So it is desirable to broaden every seam as it approaches the head and also as it approaches the foot. These cause the sail to be fuller to begin with, but as stretching proceeds it flattens out to its correct shape, i.e., the shape imparted by the curved lines drawn on the floor plan for the four sides.

Gaff mainsails are sometimes made loose-footed, the tack and clew only being attached to the boom, the object being to obtain a better setting sail. The cloths are still laid parallel to the leech, and the round of the foot is made three times as deep. This is an interesting case, as it is one of the very few where it is permissible to disobey the rule that would normally prevent the edge of a sail being cut on the cross without a bolt rope.

Here the cloths strike the foot at an angle, and yet only a tabling is fitted. The stretching allowance on the floor plan is twice that usually allowed (thus giving the same allowance as for the luff), the broad seams are made twice as wide, and the tabling is fitted on tight, all these compensating for the extra stretch by being cut on the cross. The final result is a good setting sail showing the base of each seam bending aft towards the clew. In each case the bend is more pronounced the nearer the cloth is to the clew and the points of bending, if joined, show a regularly curved line, bisecting (exactly or nearly) the clew, rising up into the sail a few feet and falling again to the tack.

* * * * *

Tools required

Needles, wax, chalk, palm, string and tape, sail hook, mallet and hammer, sharp knife.

Operation 1 The floor plan (Fig. 23). A plan of the sail is first drawn on the floor, the exact size and shape that the sail is finally required to be, except that each side is shorter by the appropriate stretching allowance, as given at the end of Chapter 2, remembering that the leech is cut parallel with the weave and the other sides, except the foot, requiring double allowance, being cut on the cross.

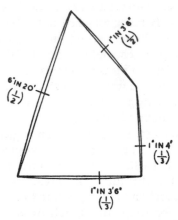

FIG. 23. Floor plan of the gaff mainsail. The depths of the curves as shown and the fractions in brackets indicate the depth along the side from the end, i.e. the maximum depth of the luff curve occurs one third of the way from the tack.

The easiest way to draw the plan is to start with the foot. Mark the appropriate tack angle (usually 85°) and draw the luff along the right hand side of the floor when standing below the foot. Using chalk and string as a compass, with centre at the top of the luff and radius that required for the head, draw an arc covering the position where the peak is expected to be. Again with centre at the clew and radius that of the leech, draw another arc to cut the first. Join the point of intersection both to the throat and clew. (*Note:* the stretching allowance for the foot is normally the same as for the leech, unless the boom is fitted with a powerful outhaul, when the allowance may be the same as the luff. If the sail is to be loose-footed, the foot allowance should be doubled, i.e. the same as the luff. If flax is used, it is usually desirable to make the allowance for the foot a little larger still.)

Having completed the drawing of the straight lines of the four sides, it is now required to draw in the curves. These are all convex (curving outwards), the maximum depth of each being as follows: Luff — 1 in. in 4 ft.; head — 1 in. in 3 ft. 6 in.; leech — 6 in. in 20 ft.; foot — 1 in. in 3 ft. 6in. (3 in. in 3 ft. 6 in. if loose-footed). The maximum depth of the curve in each case will be: Luff — one-third up; head — midway; leech — midway; foot — one-third way along from tack. Having fixed the position of maximum depth, draw in the curves from each end of each straight line, passing through these points in such a way as the curves are fair, even and smooth (check each curve by looking along it with the eye at ground level).

Operation 2 Laying the cloth. First draw a line parallel to the straight line of the leech, outside it, and 2 in. away (this measurement is for small sails and should be scaled up in proportion for larger ones). Lay the first cloth with the selvedge edge along this line, covering the curved line of the leech, starting at the clew (overlapping the curved line of the foot by 3½ in.). Cut the cloth from the roll parallel with the head, leaving 3½ in. overlapping the curved line of the head (Fig. 24). Mark in the seam line along the inner edge of the cloth, this line gradually moving further from the edge of the cloth at each end to form the broad-seams.

G

Note on broad-seams. The broad-seam is designed to allow for the additional stretch caused by cutting the material on the cross, and is made by increasing the overlap of the cloths towards each end of each cloth. The sew-

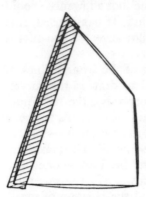

FIG. 24. Laying the first cloth of the gaff mainsail. The shaded portion indicates the first cloth.

ing guide just drawn, therefore, moves further from the edge very gradually, the seam starting to widen 18 in. for 20 ft. of leech from the head, and 3 ft. for the same at the foot (e.g. if the leech of the sail is 30 ft., the seams at the head would start broadening 2 ft. 3 in. below the gaff, and 4 ft. 6 in. above the foot). In small sails of say 150 sq. ft. the normal width of seam will be ½ in. This would be increased in proportion as the sail gets larger. At the head each seam should broaden so that it becomes half as wide again as the ordinary seam. At the foot each seam should broaden to twice as wide. In the case of a loose-foot the broad-seams should be twice as wide as broad-seams would normally be when a bolt rope is fitted, and should reach up half as high again.

The cloth will already have been false seamed if 36 in. wide cloth is being used. Except in very small sails, one false-seam is enough producing cloths 18 in. wide. In flax sails, where the material usually comes in 24 in. wide, it is quite in order to have 2 ft. wide cloths, except again in small sails which should then be fitted with 12 in. cloths.

If there are false-seams, it will not of course be possible

to broaden every seam. This will not matter in small sails, but in larger ones it is better to use narrower cloth that does not require false seaming.

Having drawn in the sewing guide on the first cloth, broadening each end as required, lay the edge of the next cloth along the guide, starting at the head with the end just cut from the first cloth, with the cloth the same way up, and overlapping the curved line of the head by the same amount (the cloth thus fitting almost exactly with none cut to waste). Carry on with the third cloth in exactly the same way, starting this time from the foot, where again there should be no waste, and so on until the whole plan is covered.

Next place the strike-up marks at about 1 ft. intervals in pencil across every seam, half the mark being on one cloth and half on the other (these are to be matched up in the stitching of the cloth). Next lift the leech cloth and place apart, place the next cloth on it the same way round, then the next until all are in one pile, with the luff cloth on top.

Operation 3 Sewing the cloths. Refer to page 71 describing this exact operation for the Bermudian mainsail. The same instructions apply.

Operation 4 Patches and Tablings. Refer to instructions for carrying out these operations on the Bermudian mainsail on pages 71–72. The patches for each corner are shaped as in Fig. 25, though of course the shapes may vary to individual taste. (The measurements apply to small sails of about 150 sq. ft. and should be scaled up for larger sails.) Apart from the shape, the patches are fitted exactly as for the Bermudian mainsails.

Tablings. These are fitted in exactly the same way as described on pages 71–72. All are cut and resewn in the same way except that the leech tabling may be turned in double without being first cut, i.e. the cloth should be turned in at the curved line of the leech, and turned in again to finish the proper width of the tabling (the last part going to the edge of the sail, so that the tabling finishes with three thicknesses, or two thicknesses in addition to the sail),

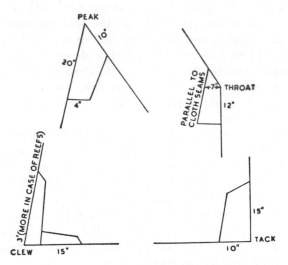

FIG. 25. Patches of the gaff mainsail. The measurements shown are for an average gaff mainsail of 150 sq. ft.

then sew down as usual with two rows of stitching. For small sails of about 150 sq. ft. the widths of the tablings should finish as follows: Luff 2½ in., foot 1½ in., leech 1 in., head 2 in. As before, these measurements should be scaled in proportion for larger sail areas.

Operation 5 Roping and finishing. This is exactly as described on page 78 for the Bermudian mainsail. The size of rope to be chosen should be the same as for the Bermudian sails of the same area. All the eyelets should be sewn for maximum strength, it being usual to fit two close together for each mast hoop where these are used.

Gaff topsail

As this is a less commonly used sail, it is not proposed to describe it in detail. We would just say that it is best mitre cut, as in a foresail, and may be cut and made in just the same way, the luff being roped (make normal allowance for the luff rope to stretch on the floor plan). Alternatively the luff may be wired as in a foresail. (*Note*: The foot is usually longer than the leech.)

Gunter (or high peaked) lugsail

This is made in exactly the same way as the Bermudian mainsail, except that in the floor plan (Fig. 26) the luff

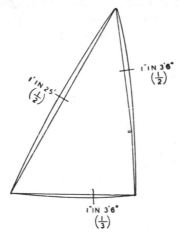

FIG. 26. Floor plan of the gunter lugsail. The depths of the curves are as shown, the fractions in brackets indicating the position of maximum depth of the curve along the side, i.e. the maximum depth of the foot curve occurs one-third of the way along from the tack.

turns through an angle of about 5° to form the head.
Make the usual allowance for stretch, and when drawing
in the curved lines of the head and luff, proceed as follows:
from half way along the head, draw outwards a distance of
1 in. in 3 ft. 6 in. Starting from the peak draw a smooth
curve passing through the point just found and finishing
at the tack (thus there will not be an angle at the throat on
the curved line of head and luff, and the distance between
the curved line and the throat angle will vary with the
angle of the head to the luff).

After this, proceed exactly as for a Bermudian mainsail,
except that normally a sewn throat eyelet is fitted the appropriate distance from the luff and head rope at the position of the angle between the straight lines of luff and head.

Fitting head and clew for luff and foot grooves. Proceed
exactly as for the Bermudian mainsail (page 79), except
that the peak will have a sewn eyelet instead of the headboard.

CHAPTER 7

THE PARACHUTE SPINNAKER

HAVING ordered a spinnaker, a yachtsman asked the sailmaker, 'How do you calculate the curve of the centre seam on the floor plan?', to which was replied, 'It's experience.' With a smile the yachtsman said, 'Oh, you mean you just guess', and the sailmaker agreed, 'Well — yes, I suppose so.'

We have laughed many times over this, as we felt that it destroyed so completely the aura of mystery with which sailmakers have always surrounded their craft, and that it rather unfairly suggested that there was really nothing clever about it. The fact is, however, that the entire success of a spinnaker hinges on the guessing of the curve of the centre seam.

The floor plan, as drawn in chalk on the sail loft floor, shows only half the sail, the luff or leech being on the left (standing at the foot of the sail), and on the right the centre seam, which runs from the peak to the middle of the foot (Fig. 27). If the centre seam meets the luff at an acute angle, it will be seen immediately that the head of the sail will

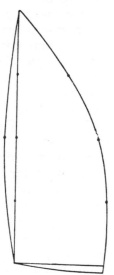

FIG. 27 Floor plan of the spinnaker, representing one half only of the sail.

91

be narrow, making the area less; but at the same time, the head of the sail is more nearly at right angles to the wind, receives more pressure from it, and lifts the remainder of the sail more strongly.

This lift is important, as stability is directly proportional to it — and stability is the keynote to any spinnaker, cruising or racing. For the cruising yacht a stable spinnaker is obviously essential, as there is nothing more uncomfortable than a spinnaker which will not stay set; and for a racing boat, the adverse effect of even a momentary collapse of the sail is remarkable. So one is reduced to a compromise — to obtain maximum area and stability at the expense of neither.

It does seem that, before the wind at any rate, the cloths of a parachute spinnaker may run in any direction, and be any width, provided that the two halves of the sail are the correct shape; for reaching, however, it is desirable to consider the matter rather more carefully. On a pure reach, the leading edge of the spinnaker is similar in operation to the luff of a Genoa, except that, being loose and in a curve, it will curl over as soon as the wind gets behind it (it is of interest to note here that it rarely appears to pay to set the spinnaker on a pure reach, and that there is often considerable advantage to be gained in taking it off in good time. The reason is clearly that, though the area of the spinnaker is far greater than that of the foresail, some of the spinnaker is actually tending to drive the yacht backwards).

The readiness of the luff to curl over and collapse the sail is dependent on the fullness of the section of the sail near the luff, and this, in turn, is influenced to some extent by the angle the cloths make to the luff. In theory, if the cloths lie at an angle to the luff, which is normally prevented from stretching by a thin wire or line, the sail in the region of the luff can be stretched a little more as the wind fills the sail, causing a little more fullness, than when the seams are at right angles, or parallel, to the luff. Again, if they are at right angles, the stretch should be less than when parallel, owing to the numerous seams running into the luff, and finally, less still if the cloths are narrow, with a greater number of seams. So we conclude that the best cut for reaching has comparatively narrow cloths at right angles to luff and leech.

This cut, known sometimes as the 'herringbone cut', appears first to have been made by the Americans, and it certainly looks attractive. We ourselves went even further, cutting a Dragon spinnaker with the cloths at right angles to the foot as well, by mitre-cutting each half of the sail, last seams each side bisecting the clews. This sail certainly seemed to do very well, though in fact we could not find any real evidence to suggest that it was really better than other cuts.

In practice it is extremely difficult to decide which cut is preferable, as it is quite noticeable that no-one seems to obtain advantage out of any particular cut — one merely seems to notice disadvantages from particular spinnakers for no apparent reason other than, perhaps, that they are unstable or too big or too small for the weather conditions at the time. Our feeling is that, provided that the shape of the sail is right, there is very little to choose between the cuts, and from the point of view of weight saving, it might be preferred to have the cloths as wide as possible.

Although it would be easy to make an unstable spinnaker, shapes and designs of stable ones may vary considerably — a statement superbly borne out by the photograph of *Caprece* racing in the 'Q' class, with the spinnaker upside down! (Plate XXXIV). The head was at the end of the boom and one of the clews was on the halyard, making a most peculiarly long footed sail, which yet set magnificently and was perfectly stable. It was most noticeable, however, that the yacht's speed was less than with the spinnaker hoisted correctly, which observation indicated clearly that, though a spinnaker may set well and be stable, it is not necessarily producing maximum results.

The shapes and sizes of spinnakers in actual use vary considerably, largely as a result of different class rules. The R.O.R.C. rule penalises a sail of width more than 1.8 times the length of the base of the fore-triangle, so that yachts racing under R.O.R.C. rules rarely set spinnakers of greater width than this which, for the average yacht, gives a sail of only moderate width. With the Metre classes, on the other hand, it is only the length of spinnaker boom and the length of the luff which are governed, so that the tendency here is to have a spinnaker as wide as will set. This produces interesting results, not least of which is that it is not necessarily the largest spinnakers which give the best results, even in light weather.

The cruising man, on the other hand, must necessarily view spinnakers from a different standpoint. Sometimes he dislikes them altogether because they tend to mean extra complication, more crew and greater expense (though, in such a case, our private feeling is that he might change his mind if he tried a spinnaker), but in any case, his main concern must be stability, both in calm and rough seas. It is essentially so, as he would not, and in fact could not, concentrate on the set of the sail in the way that class racing demands. Thus, cruising spinnakers are usually narrower and less full in the head.

The choice of material to be used would seem to lie between terylene (or dacron), nylon and Egyptian cotton.

We feel that it is true to say that terylene will produce the best results, being lighter for a given strength, and stretching least, so that whatever the wind strength, the sail will remain the same shape. Nylon is also light, but stretches considerably (this is not always detrimental, but it does mean that allowance for stretch has to be taken into consideration, as otherwise it might be that the sail is good in light winds but unstable when it blows). Egyptian cotton is less expensive, and stretches little, but has the considerable disadvantage of absorbing water and thereby increasing its already greater weight, not to mention the additional trouble involved in maintaining the sail in good condition.

Tools required

Needles, palm, wax, chalk, spike (for large spinnakers), sharp knife.

The cut for the spinnaker we have chosen to describe is, perhaps, the simplest and most inexpensive, the cloth being used full width and lying parallel to the luff and leech. For ordinary purposes there is little difference in the effectiveness of the different cuts, but if you prefer to lay the cloths a different way, this can be done without in any way upsetting the method of making the sail which, as usual, is begun with a floor plan.

Operation 1   Drawing the floor plan (Fig. 27). A plan of half the spinnaker, full size before stretching, is first drawn on the floor in chalk, the luff, represented by a straight line, being on your left as you stand at the foot, and the foot, again represented by a straight line, lying at right angles to the luff. Both the luff and foot are curved convexly, these curves being drawn as follows: Luff. The curve is regular, the deepest point being drawn midway along the luff, the depth being equivalent to 3 in. for every 5 ft. of luff (i.e. 12 in. for a luff of 20 ft.) The foot also has a regular curve, with maximum depth 6 in. for every 10 ft. of foot, but as the foot line is the length of only half the foot, the curve will join the tack to a point representing the maximum depth. (Care should be taken here that when the spinnaker is opened out, the curve will be a fair one, by ensuring that, at the centre point, the line of the curve is horizontal.)

The third side of the diagram represents the centre seam which, as explained, is of vital importance. To find it, divide the luff into four equal parts, and from the point a quarter way down, measure to the right, from the curved line of the luff, a distance equal to three-fifths of the length of the foot line. At the half-way mark, again from the curve of the luff, measure the same length as the foot line, and at the three-quarter mark $1\frac{1}{20}$ the length of the foot line. Now join the peak to the right hand end of the curved foot line, by laying the tape measure, or something similar, along the points just found. As it is not entirely easy to see how fair the curve in fact is, it is desirable to take great care to get it just right, looking at the curve from every angle.

When you are satisfied, move the foot of the tape to the left an amount equal to $1\frac{1}{2}$ in. per 10 ft. of foot in such a way as to keep the fairness of the curve. This movement will draw the foot in slightly to prevent the round on the foot becoming slack. When you are finally satisfied, draw a chalk line where the tape has lain. To complete the floor plan, measure from the centre of the curved luff line to the left 2 in. and through the point found, draw a straight line parallel to the straight line of the luff and the same length.

Operation 2   Laying the cloth. Lay the first cloth (Fig. 28) with its edge along this line and with the end of the cloth overlapping the curved line of the foot by not less than 1 in. Cut off the roll so that the cloth overlaps the centre seam line by ¾ in. Along the right hand edge of the first cloth, draw a sewing guide in pencil ½ in. in from the edge. Now, turning the remainder of the material round, but not over, and starting from the top, lay the second cloth so that it overlaps the first, the edge lying along the sewing guide (maintaining the same overlaps at the centre seam and foot).

Continue laying the cloths until the plan is covered (small spinnakers may have as few as two cloths, but this is quite in order). Mark next intermittent pencil lines on the cloth to correspond with the curved luff lines, by turning the edge up. Place the strike-up marks in pencil at 1 ft. intervals across every seam and then lift the right hand cloth, place apart on the floor, and place each cloth in turn on it, so that a pile is formed with the left-hand cloth on top.

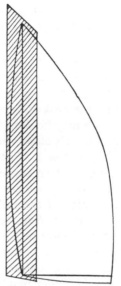

FIG. 28. Laying the first cloth of the spinnaker, the shaded portion representing the first cloth.

As only half of the spinnaker has been laid, the other half should be laid and cut on the same floor plan in exactly the same way, and piled as before. Time may be saved by laying the second half on top of the first.

Operation 3 Sewing the cloths. The cloths are sewn, either with a straight or cross stitch, using a flat seam, in exactly the same way as for foresail and mainsail, starting with the first two from one of the piles, seeing that the bulk of the sail is to the left of the machine and that the two halves of the strike-up marks match in each case. When the two halves of the sail have been sewn, they are sewn together along the centre seam. Although it is not a vital matter, it is desirable that the seams each side should meet on the centre seam, and of course, it is necessary that the peak and foot should match exactly after sewing, which may be done by marking the two halves of the sail at intervals along the seam before sewing.

Operation 4   Fitting patches (Fig. 29). These are required at each corner of the sail, and are made as follows: Spread out each corner in turn, and with centre at the intersection of the luff and foot or leech lines, draw an arc (with radius 6 in. for spinnakers up to 100 sq. ft. scaling up in proportion for larger sails), cutting the luff and foot lines. This represents the outer patch. Now reduce the radius by one-third and draw another similar arc to indicate the under patch. Cut out the under patches from the spare cloth, so that they exactly fit the triangle formed by the arc, making sure that the weave of the cloth is the same as that in the sail. Sew these under patches on with a row of stitches $\frac{1}{4}$ in. from the arc, leaving the other two sides of each patch unsewn.

Next cut the larger patches in the same way but leaving an extra $\frac{1}{2}$ in. of cloth along the arc side for turning in. Sew these patches to the sail with a line of stitching along the arc so that the edge of the patch is turned in and under and lies along the line of the arc. The other two sides of both the under and top patches will be sewn automatically with the finishing of the sides of the sail.

Operation 5   Fitting the tablings. These tablings are formed by turning in the cloth double along the pencil line, but reinforced by tape as well. Having creased the cloth along the pencil line, open the cloth out again and sew 2 in. tape (coloured if desired) on the underneath side

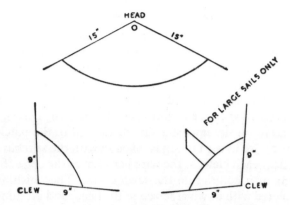

FIG. 29. Patches of the parachute spinnaker. The sizes
shown are for an average sail of 250 sq. ft.

of the cloth, so that the crease line runs exactly down the
middle of the tape, and when the cloth is folded over
again, half the tape will show and half will still be underneath. Now turn in the edge of the cloth, so that the
tabling finishes 1 in. wide, i.e., half the width of the tape,
and sew the tabling down with two rows of stitching,
close to each side of the tabling.

It is advantageous to have the tape on each of the three
sides different colours, to assist in setting. The width of
the tape may be reduced for small spinnakers, and for
larger ones, say over 400 sq. ft., a thin wire is fitted in the
luff and leech. To fit this wire, splice a loop in the end to
fit the sewn eyelet in the clew, and sew it in with the eyelet.
The wire is then made to run, in the tabling, to the peak
and down again to the other clew, finishing in the eyelet
in the same way.

It is necessary to prevent the sail sliding up and down
the wire by sewing through the wire at 2 ft. intervals, in
such a way as to hold the wire into the very edge of the
sail. The wire is then finally held into the edge of the
tabling, either by sewing with the machine, fitted with a
special piping foot, or by hand with the sticking stitch.

Operation 6   Finishing. For small sails, this is simply done by fitting a sewn eyelet at each corner, $\frac{1}{2}$ in. in from the edges, but large spinnakers require roping at the three corners with thin Italian hemp (say $\frac{3}{4}$ in. circumference), for about 18 in. either side of the eyelet in each case. The rope is tailed at each end and sewn as previously described. It is sewn on the opposite side of the sail to the patches, and the wire in the tabling is taken in with the stitches except near each clew, as the wire here leaves the edge of the tabling as it comes into the sewn eyelet. The finishing is completed with a swivel seized to the head, and grommets, either served wire, or rope, fitted in each clew.

Orbital-cut spinnakers

It is popular these days to cut spinnakers without a vertical centre seam, and with horizontal cloths, the shape of the spinnaker being induced by tapering each cloth individually towards each leech. The object is to make a spinnaker of given width set flatter and wider thus, in theory at least, being more efficient both on the reach and on the run. But, whereas the vertical centre seam spinnaker described will work well for all, the orbital spinnaker is treacherous ground, the design having to be perfected for every individual spinnaker except its twin. If the design is not quite right the spinnaker is likely to be unsatisfactory.

So it is that while a sailmaker specialising in the spinnakers of a particular one-design class may perfect a design so that each spinnaker produced is good, the home sailmaker is not likely to make enough of one spinnaker to have a chance of getting the sail just right, and for this reason we offer the vertical centre seam spinnaker, and leave it to readers to design the orbital spinnakers themselves if they desire, using as a pattern, if possible, an existing spinnaker of similar size and known efficiency.

CHAPTER 8

STORMSAILS

Trysail

THIS varies in style considerably, but in all cases is made as strongly as possible throughout. It is fitted to the mast in the normal way, and is either sheeted as foresail quite independently of the boom, or is fitted to the boom either by slides all along the foot, or as a loose-footed sail, attached to the boom at the clew. Thus there is a considerable range to choose from, and the choice will depend on the type of vessel, the use to which it is put, and personal preference.

The most usual form of trysail is that whose tack is a few feet above the boom and whose clew droops to a position below the boom, being sheeted on the leeward side of the deck. This sail is best cut parallel with the leech, the cloths being laid as for the gaff sail (page 84). The same curve as for a loose-footed gaff sail is required, the foot being broad seamed in exactly the same way. The luff and leech are both treated in the same way as for a gaff sail.

As a general guide the cloth should be twice as heavy as that required for the same size mainsail and eyelets, seams, bolt ropes, etc., twice as large and strong. It is desirable to rope the sail all the way round. The same large size rope may be used all the way, but, for convenience in handling, it is desirable to use rope of half the diameter for the leech and foot, that is, between points a few feet inwards from tack and clew and from head and clew (so that the tack, head and clew are all fitted with the larger rope). In each case the smaller rope is fitted to the larger with long splices.

Storm Foresails

These are made in exactly the same way as ordinary ones except that, as with trysails, they are made twice as strong, and are best roped all round.

Comparative sizes

Though the matter is largely one of choice, the average storm sails compare approximately with full sized sails as follows:

Bermudian mainsail. Reduce luff and foot by one-third (by three-quarters in the case of the foot of a trysail whose clew sets below the level of the boom).

Foresail. With the same luff, reduce the last seam by one-third, making the storm foresail a narrower shape.

In the case of other rigs, the same area reduction should be satisfactory.

CHAPTER 9

THE STRETCHING OF NEW SAILS, THEIR CARE AND MAINTENANCE

Stretching (cotton and flax)

THE object of careful stretching of sails is to ensure that the canvas stretches evenly all over until it reaches its normal working area. Generally speaking the more expensive the cloth, the tighter will be the weave and the less the stretch, but all cotton sailcloths will stretch a certain amount, and all in the normal way reach a point beyond which they will not stretch unless unreasonably forced to do so.

Sail stretching can be compared to running in an engine in that careful stretching in the first place pays handsome dividends later; that is, stretching both carefully *and* correctly. The strain on the canvas must be smooth and evenly distributed, light winds being preferable in achieving this. Rain and spray are most undesirable in tending to cause uneven contractions.

Thus it is best to choose a fine, calm and dry day. The foresail luff should be stretched tight in the normal way, as the luff wire will not alter in length and the luff is made to the correct length in the first place. The clew should be sheeted correctly, at a position on the deck just forward of the point that the production of the last seam would strike (the exact point can be found by standing on the sheet whilst under way and adjusting the foot until the correct setting is achieved). Use the sail in this way for the first few sails and it will give no trouble. Do not worry too much if the conditions are not ideal, as fore-sails and genoas do not spoil very easily.

Greater attention should be paid to the Bermudian mainsail, if a perfect shape is to be achieved. There are two stretching factors to be considered, the rope and the sailcloth. Where the cloth is cut on the cross, the rope is fitted to prevent the cloth from stretching by virtue of being cut on the cross, but allowing the normal stretch of the yarns. As the rope stretches considerably more than the yarns, it is put on tight so that, when fully stretched, the yarns of the cloth are also fully stretched.

As the reason for stretching the sail carefully is to ensure that the stretching force is applied evenly, there is ob-viously no harm in stretching out the rope immediately until it is the same length as the unstretched canvas — in fact, there may be harm in not doing so as the boom would be found to droop, putting undue strain on the leech, leaving the luff baggy, thereby tending to stretch the sail unevenly. So it is desirable to stretch the luff *and* foot ropes out until puckers in the canvas disappear, when the canvas will then be properly set in an unstretched condition. As the sail is used, the luff and foot ropes should be stretched gradually until they come out to their fully stretched lengths.

In general it is undesirable to reef a mainsail until it is fully stretched, though if the reef is tied perfectly it should not be injurious. Owing to the fact that the cloth is subject to more stretch than a fully stretched sail, any localised strain will have much greater effect and the girts produced in the canvas by incorrect reefing will be more pro-nounced, and might be permanent.

A truly tied reef will spread the load evenly, and should

not cause harm except in so far as that, all the time the reefed sail is in use, the portion above the reef is being stretched and that below is not. If the reefed sail is used for long, the difference in stretching of the two parts is bound to show, setting badly in the same way as a sail half wet, the dry part being normal, the wet part having shrunk.

In the normal way, of course, there should be no temptation to reef, as conditions in which it would be necessary would be most unsuitable for sail stretching.

Spinnakers do not in the normal way require any special treatment when new, though it is desirable to be on the safe side by setting them first in reasonable conditions.

Terylene sails are ordinarily made full size, and do not need any initial stretching. Care, however, should be taken initially while the stitching settles down to its permanent position.

To avoid over-stretching sails, it is most desirable to paint black bands on mast and boom to show exactly where peak and clew should lie when the sail is set, and every time to set the sail to them exactly.

Maintaining correct set of the sails (cotton and flax)
It is a fact that many boats are fitted with means, such as a winch or a purchase, of hoisting the luff of a mainsail really tight, and yet are not similarly equipped for the foot. Where this is the case, we would ask you to beware of having the luff too tight, as the set of the sail may be spoilt by the appearance of a ridge running along the base ends of the battens, a fault which is not very easy to correct.

Apart from the desirability of having the foot outhaul purchase to match that of the main halyard, it is often necessary to be able to haul out hard on the clew, as when the foot rope has been slacked off and has become wet overnight. If the mainsail is to set properly, the canvas must be stretched out to its normal tightness. The canvas will have contracted slightly, so that the foot of the sail will be a little shorter (say an inch in 10 ft., depending on the style of the cloth), but the rope may have shrunk some five times as much, needing considerable power to increase its length to that of the shrunk length of the sail. If the purchase is powerful enough, it would be possible to break the rope, unless care is taken not to stretch it out too suddenly. The same procedure is required equally for the luff, but here the purchase is usually more than sufficient.

In order to maintain the correct set of the mainsail, it will be necessary to stretch the luff and foot, when these are dry, a little more, to take up the increase in length of the canvas caused by drying. Often the vessel is already underway before the foot of the sail is dry, and with the weight of the boom on the sail, a powerful purchase, operated from the mast, will be necessary to take the clew finally to its proper mark.

Theoretically, if one stretches out a rope when wet to the same length it was when dry, it will relax afterwards into a slightly longer length than before, which would tend to make the sail gradually larger. With care, however, this difficulty will not be experienced in practice.

For a given length, a thicker rope will stretch more than a thinner one (though it will need more power), so that if the bolt rope is a thick one, it will be easier to stretch it out to the required length when wet, and there would be less chance of breaking it.

Although on small yachts it is not essential to slack off the luff and foot ropes when these are wetted, more care is necessary in larger yachts. And in very large ones the strain set up in the bolt ropes by being wetted can be such that the ropes can break if they are not slacked off at all.

Genoas provide less of a problem, as the wire luff is fixed in length, and the leech and foot are free. It is merely desirable to ensure that the clew is correctly sheeted to avoid the possibility of the sail being stretched unfairly. Spinnakers again require no special treatment.

Maintaining the canvas in good condition (*cotton and flax*)

When new, sailcloth will become mildewed under very slight provocation, the most ideal conditions being warmth and damp together, without free passage of air (as when the sails are packed wet in the bag and left under the deck in hot weather). It is therefore desirable to have the sail mildew proofed either in the cloth before the sail is made up, or after the sail is finished. The latter method has an advantage in that the stitching and rope, etc., is proofed in addition to the canvas, but all the same we would recommend the former (which is in fact more popular) as it is undesirable in principle to process a new sail at all, and it is much easier and more convenient to buy the cloth already proofed.

If the cloth is not mildew-proofed, great care should be taken to see that it is never left wet for long. If it is mildew-proofed, less care is needed; but if facilities for drying are not available, it is good to have the sail made water repellant, as well as being mildew-proofed, as this will give maximum protection.

In the case of terylene and nylon, none of these precautions is necessary as, though it may be possible to mildew them, this is not easy.

Washing sails (cotton and flax)

When sails are soaked in seawater and dried, a deposit
of salt is left in the fibres. The salt being hygroscopic (i.e.
tending to absorb moisture) the sail will become damp
again automatically unless, which is hardly ever the case,
there is no moisture in the atmosphere. And as soon as it is
damp it will tend to rot. Thus it is essential to wash the
sail in fresh water before storing, making sure that all the
salt has been dissolved by the water. If there is much salt
in the sail, a very thorough wash will be required, perhaps
in more than one lot of fresh water. When the sail is dry
and is free from salt, it will no longer feel stiff.

To get the best out of a sail, it is desirable to wash it
periodically during the season in any case, as the presence
of salt causes slight contraction, and the stiffness will
spoil the set in light weather.

Care should be taken not to launder the sails or treat
them with chemicals, as the solidity of the cloth will be
lessened, and in some cases sailcloth may even come to
look more like calico.

It is always necessary to grease slides periodically, but
if grease is allowed to stain the canvas, difficulty may be
experienced in removing the marks completely. The normal method of removing stains is by using 'Thawpit' or a
similar carbon tetrachloride cleaner, washing afterwards
in fresh water. Put a clean pad under the part to be cleaned
to absorb the dissolved grease, so that it does not spread
over a larger area of the sail.

Avoiding chafe (cotton and flax)

Chafe usually occurs by the vessel rolling in a calm, the
sails slatting about and chafing on the rigging, particularly

the running stays. This should be minimised, as far as possible, and the seam stitching inspected afterwards.

Sometimes the headboard may foul the back stay by being hoisted too high. This may cause chafe of the bolt rope.

Where shackles are used to secure the slides, it is necessary to protect the bolt rope in way of each shackle with raw-hide, as otherwise the shackles will chafe the rope every time the yacht goes about.

Terylene (Dacron) sails

To maintain these in good condition it is essential from the first moment of use to set them exactly to the designed lengths on the spars, to avoid leaving them exposed to sunlight for long periods, and to beware particularly of chafe. If the sails are left wet in a very warm, damp atmosphere, mildew can disfigure them but will not damage them.

As polyester fibre sailcloth is much harder than cloths made of natural fibres the stitching of the seams tends to remain proud, and is therefore more vulnerable to chafe against rigging, etc. Sails should periodically be examined for this, particularly in the parts most likely to come into contact with rigging, spars, etc.

CHAPTER 10

RENOVATION, REPAIR
AND ALTERATION

*Renovation of sails — restoring to old sails the shape they had
when new.*

THIS is an important repair which may save the buy-
ing of a new sail if the existing one should no longer
be setting properly. It is based on the principle that,
provided the sail may be stretched out flat on the floor,
it must be possible to alter it in such a way that it has the
shape of a similar new sail, even if, as will sometimes be
the case, the sail after alteration is a trace smaller than it
was before.

First remove the luff and foot rope to enable the canvas
to be laid out flat, having previously marked the rope all
along its full length with a straight line in pencil parallel to
the tabling, and having placed marks at frequent intervals
(say 6 in.) across the rope and tabling to ensure that the
rope can be replaced in the same position as before.

Next spread the sail out flat on the floor, fixing it with
pins or weights in such a way that it is absolutely flat in its
natural shape, without wrinkles and as far as possible
stretched at even tension all over (fixing it in its natural
position is most important, as otherwise it would be quite
easy to increase the round of the leech at the expense of the
luff and vice versa). Then, using thread stretched tight
between head and tack, head and clew and tack and clew,
show the position of the straight lines of a floor plan of a

new sail which would be made to the size of the present sail before stretching. Draw in the curves of the luff, leech and foot as per instructions for new sails, but making the depth of the leech curve only $\frac{2}{3}$ the depth of the leech curve for a new sail (this is because the sail is already stretched).

Measure the width of the tabling, and along luff and foot draw a line inside the floorplan curves of luff and foot and parallel to them the exact width of the tabling away from them. Now move the tabling inwards until its inner edge lies over the line just drawn (leaving a pleat underneath), and sew down with one line of stitching. If the pleat underneath is small, it may be sewn straight down to the tabling with a second line of stitching. If large it should be cut so that the under piece is half an inch or so (depending on the size of the sail) from the first line of stitching, and the outer piece double the width. Turn this in and sew down with a second line of stitching, making a neat seam. Usually the pleat will taper to nothing at each end, so that the pleat should not be cut until it becomes too wide for sewing down without cutting.

On some sails it will be found that the leech tabling is sewn on separately, having been fitted a little tighter than the edge of the sail to allow for stretch. This should be removed and resewn in the new position. It may be that, apart from a short length at the lower end of the leech, it is not desired to make an alteration, in which case it is merely necessary to remove and refit the lower end of the tabling only (this correction would be due to the foot having been stretched). This involves the cutting off of the clew eyelet, when new patches should be made and fitted, and a new sewn eyelet worked in.

In the event of the sail being too flat, so that it is necessary to increase the depths of the rounds on luff and foot, the alteration will of necessity decrease the lengths of luff and foot. In this case, the straight lines should be placed far enough in from the existing edges to allow of the drawing of the proper luff and foot curves (the flatter the sail is, the further in will the straight lines be placed). First remove the headboard and refit in the new position as described later in this chapter, cutting the tabling off from luff and foot, lifting the tack patches either side and leaving them intact, attached to the tabling. Sew the tabling down to the sail the same way as before, turning in the cloth underneath to make a neat seam, sewing the tack patches in the new position.

Having carried out the necessary alteration, resew the rope, making sure that it is fitted exactly as before.

In general this method of restoration should apply satisfactorily in all cases except where, for some reason, the sail will not lie flat on the floor in its natural position. If this should be found to be so, the difficulty might be solved by the insertion of a new piece of cloth, but of course each case would have to be judged on its merits. A parachute spinnaker would certainly not lie flat on the floor, as it is extremely bowl-shaped, but here it is merely necessary to take the two halves apart up the centre seam, correcting each half separately.

In the case of foresails with wire luffs, it is desirable to remove the wire as it will be found much easier to work with it out. This is not essential, however, as the wire does not stretch or contract.

The most common fault which this method of renovation will be required to cure is over-fullness in the flow of the sail, caused by the stretching of the material. This will be particularly noticeable in the luff when close-hauled, as it will be found that when the yacht is pointing normally, the luff is lifting, whereas in fact it should be just on the point of lifting but not actually doing so. It should not, however, be assumed that in this case the sail is cut too full, as it could be caused by the luff rope having been fitted too tight or even by the thin wire fitted in the luff to prevent over stretching not being slack enough to allow the rope to stretch to its proper length. But whatever the cause it will be apparent as soon as the rope is removed.

A fault which is perhaps a little more difficult to cure is a ridge in the sail running along the feet of the battens, caused by overstretching the luff. The obvious cure for this is to overstretch the foot as well, but this is usually impracticable. The cure may, however, be affected by reducing the curve of the leech and setting the battens further into the sail, in addition to reshaping the sail.

When the renovation has been completed, it must be remembered that the actual sail is no longer sewn to the rope, but is joined to the tabling by two rows of stitching, which will be of quite sufficient strength provided it is maintained in good condition.

To decide whether a repair is justified

This will depend largely on how extensive is the proposed repair. A little repair might be justified on a sail in bad condition where such repair as a renewal of a whole cloth would not be contemplated. So the decision is a matter for one's own judgement, based on knowledge of sailmaking procedure to estimate the extent of the repair, and on the assessment of the condition of the sail.

In the normal way it will be found that the sewing machine stitching rots more quickly than the canvas, so that re-sewing seams which have parted is a common repair. It should not be assumed that if the thread is weak the canvas will be also. (If the seams should be found to be giving way in different parts of the sail, it is usually desirable to put an extra line of stitching along every seam between the two existing rows, using either straight or cross stitch.)

Before proceeding with any repair, it is desirable to find out what the actual cloth is like, and this is most simply done by pricking it with a needle. If the needle gradually passes through the cloth under continuous pressure, parting the strands as it goes, then the cloth is good and strong. If, however, it makes a pop as it enters the cloth, breaking a strand, going through easily and leaving a large hole, then the cloth can be judged to be very weak and nearing the end of its useful life. (Sails in this condition, especially heavy ones, may yet last a long time, but, like motoring with a smooth tyre, there is a risk. If, for instance, a sharp fitting should make a small hole in the canvas, this might result in splitting the sail in half, instead of staying, in a good sail, as a small hole.) Occasionally one comes across sails which look in excellent condition but which are, in fact, completely rotten. The treatments of oil and ochre, which gives a brown rather sticky appearance, and of cutch tanning, producing a brown matt finish, are sometimes given to sails which are already rotten, with the result that they look splendid, but in fact are in no better condition than they were before.

Patching

If possible, patches should be made of the same material as the sail, and in the same condition. They should also always be rectangular, whatever the shape of the hole or tear.

First cut out a rectangle of cloth of size and shape sufficient to cover the damaged area comfortably, making sure that the weave of the cloth is at right angles to the edges of the patch and that the weave of the patch will exactly coincide with the weave of the sail. Place the patch in position, turn in the edges all round, draw a line on the sail round the patch the exact shape of the patch, and place strike-up marks across the edges of the patch at frequent intervals, making one of them double so that the patch can be replaced in the same position without difficulty when under the machine.

Sew the patch to the sail with one line of stitching close to the edge of the patch, ensuring that the strike-up marks match up and that the patch is exactly sewn as previously positioned. The double strike-up mark forms a convenient starting point. Next turn the sail over and cut out the damaged cloth from under the patch leaving a margin round the edge for turning in. Turn this edge in all round, cutting at the corners as necessary, and sew down with a second line of stitching parallel to the first and as close to it as convenient.

If new cloth should be used to patch an old sail, it is necessary to allow for the fact that the new cloth will shrink a little when first put into use, and being set in cloth which has already stretched to its normal limit, there will be no force on the patch to stretch it again, with the result that if allowance is not made, puckers will show, radiating from the patch. The difficulty is overcome by making the patch a little too large, say $\frac{1}{4}$ in. in a 4 in. patch. The extra $\frac{1}{4}$ in. is taken in evenly all round before placing the strike-up marks, which, when matched, ensure that the extra cloth is sewn in evenly.

Sometimes the patch will require to overlap a seam or

tabling, in which case it is first necessary to lift the tabling (or adjoining cloth) sew the patch as before, and then re-sew tabling or seam, arranging if possible that the edge of the patch which lies along seam or tabling is a selvedge edge, to make the job as neat as possible. If the seam should be a false one, then the patch must be sewn over it, particularly in this case ensuring that the patch has a selvedge edge. Where a new cloth is fitted near the clew, it should be treated as a patch rather than as a new cloth owing to the short length and comparative lack of strain.

Fitting new cloths

Where the damage is more extensive, it may be de-sirable to fit a whole or part new cloth. Again, if possible the same material as the sail should be used, but it is normally quite in order to use new sailcloth of the same weight. Unlike patches, a new cloth will stretch in the same way as the whole sail did originally and therefore has to be put in tight, not loose — or in other words, when the new cloth is being marked up, the sail either side of it is gathered a little to make the necessary allowance.

A new cloth is put in in just the same way as a patch, the seams either side being opened. Assuming a whole new cloth is being fitted, the allowance for its stretching would be the same as for a leech of a sail in the same cloth (see Chapter 2 for stretching allowances). Assuming this to be 6 in. in 20 ft., and the new cloth 10 ft. long, an allowance of 3 in. would be made, i.e. the new cloth would be cut 3 in. shorter than the cloths either side.

If on the other hand a half cloth is being fitted — a cloth that runs from one side of the sail to the middle of it, for half the length of the original cloth, there will be less force stretching the new cloth, and so the allowance will not be halved, but will approximately be only one-third, i.e. in this case, 1 in. in 5 ft.

If the length of the new cloth is shorter still, say 1 ft., the allowance will dwindle practically to nothing. But when the new cloth is not only a short length but is in the middle of the old cloth as well, allowance must be made the opposite way as the new length of cloth is now a patch and has to be treated as such. Whether the new cloth is treated normally or as a patch is decided upon whether the new cloth runs out to the edge of the sail. If it does not, it should be treated as a patch, though, where it approaches close to the edge of the sail there will naturally be some tendency to stretch the cloth. It will then be a case of conflicting forces, and the allowance must be judged for each individual case.

These remarks apply generally to all types of sailcloth, but in the case of terylene, no stretching allowances are necessary as the stretch of the cloth is virtually nil.

Re-setting the headboard of a Bermudian mainsail

If the canvas round the headboard is chafed and in need of repair, it is quite a simple matter to re-set the headboard. First remove the headboard from the sail, and separate the head patch from the sail with the exception of the stitching along its base. Now fit a new patch (and under patch) either side of the sail, stitching them a little below the original patch to hide the previous stitch holes, and making the patch one side finish at a slightly different level (say $1\frac{1}{2}$ in.) from the other side to enable the two patches to be put on one at a time (put the upper one on first).

The original patch and sail which previously set either side of the headboard are still in position underneath the new patches, and will have the shape of the headboard

I

clearly imprinted on them, complete with all the sewing holes. If you proceed to mark these sewing holes on to the inside of the new patches by tracing through the old canvas, and then make equivalent holes in the new canvas where you have marked, it can be ensured that the headboard can be refitted in exactly the same position as before. Having marked the new canvas, cut out the old, and set in the headboard as explained in Chapter 5.

Checking Batten Pockets

If you are overhauling your sails during the winter, and wish to make sure that they are in perfect condition, it is worth ensuring that the stitching of the seam under the batten pocket is in good order. This may be deceptive, as the batten is inclined to wear the stitching on the inside, leaving it to all appearances in good condition on the outside. To test the stitching, however, merely insert a fine spike and if the stitching is worn, it will come away easily.

To resew by machine it is necessary first to remove the batten pocket, but the seam may be resewn by hand from the outside without removing the pocket, having first inserted the batten to prevent the needle picking up the cloth of the batten pocket.

Re-wiring headsails

Re-wiring the luffs of headsails is usually necessary because the galvanising has gone from the wire and rust has set in. This normally occurs at the tack, which receives most spray. The first sign that anything is amiss is usually the appearance of rust marks on the canvas covering the wire. By then the wire will be quite rusty and if bent sharply will creak in a way that wire in good condition will not.

First cut the tabling as close to the wire as possible, unpicking the tack eye if this should be sewn into the sail. Make up the new wire to the exact length of the old, and fit to the sail a new tabling of either a wide webbing tape (say 4 in.) or a strip of canvas. The method is to crease the tabling for the whole length exactly down the middle, sew one side to the sail so that the edge lies along the edge of the old tabling (or further into the sail). Place a string inside the tabling, cut away the surplus cloth of the old tabling, leaving a good margin. Bend the new tabling over and sew it down with another row of stitches, so that the second edge is nearer to the wire than the first by $\frac{1}{4}$ in.–$\frac{1}{2}$ in., ensuring that the second line of stitching goes through both the old and the new tabling. Attach the string to the wire and pull through into the tabling, and finish off as for making a new sail.

It is to be recommended that a luff wire should be renewed as soon as rust marks appear through the canvas, otherwise there is a risk of the wire parting while under way.

Homeward bounders

This is a name given by professional sailors to temporary sail repairs good enough just to get the ship home. For instance, a patch may be fitted merely by placing over the hole or tear, sewn on by a sticking stitch round the hole, leaving the edges of the patch raw.

For a very small hole a darn would be sufficient. For a short tear a herringbone stitch darn is adequate. And for other repairs it is just a question of making sure that the method used gives enough strength, even if only temporarily.

Repairs to boltropes

Where one strand only requires renewal, cut this strand and cut the stitching attaching the rope to the sail for a distance of one foot back either way from this point, and unlay the bad strand for this distance. Lay in a new strand taken from a spare piece of rope, leaving at least 4 in. spare at each end (whilst laying up, the strand should be twisted the opposite way to the lay of the rope, as tightly as possible). Lastly, tie the two pairs of ends together and finish as in a long splice.

Renewal of a section of the bolt rope. Cut the stitching attaching the rope to the sail as far as is necessary, and cut out the section of rope that requires replacement. If the repair is fairly near the end of the rope, it is better to carry the new piece to the end, making a tail at the end. In this case, attach the new rope to the old with a long splice and re-sew to the sail. Where the repair comes in the middle of the rope, a new piece is inserted by two long splices, making sure that the finished rope is exactly the same length as before, and if a brand new piece of rope is used, allowing for same to stretch. This is rather a difficult operation to get exactly right, and it is usually worth carrying the new rope to the end, even if this should use more rope.

Enlarging and cutting down sails

It is often desired to enlarge or reduce the areas of sails, but although this is practicable in some cases, these are disappointingly few, especially as regards enlarging, where it is usually better to renew the sail. However, there are times when something can be done advantageously, and so we list the possibilities below:

Before dealing with each type of sail, there are certain

general principles which should be borne in mind. The restricting factor in nearly every case is the necessity of making sure that the cloths are still correctly laid after the alteration has been completed (in a general way, the matter is described in Chapter 1). Knowing the different practicable ways of laying the cloth, it can easily be seen from a paper drawing whether or not the new sail you want will be correctly laid. If this is found definitely not to be so, then perhaps you may be able to alter your requirements so that it would be. Sometimes, when the lay of the cloth is nearly all right, the alteration may be carried out satisfactorily by taking special precautions such as the addition of a bolt rope, or the fitting of a tight tabling, even though theoretically one should not do so. In general, however, we do recommend avoiding making alterations unless you are sure, as these are almost certain to be unsatisfactory when essential sailmaking conditions are not fulfilled.

Bermudian Mainsails (Enlarging) (Fig 30)

Assuming that the cloths are laid at right angles to the leech, there is only one practicable way of enlarging the sail, this involving making the foot and luff longer. Remove the rope from the foot and a short way up the luff, split the sail at the tack seam, lower the foot in such a way as the two parts of the leech continue in one straight line. Insert in between the two parts a new cloth (or cloths) of the width required. Continue the lines of the foot and luff to meet at the new tack, and finish as for a new sail. The old leech tabling should be entirely removed and a new one of the required length fitted (when fitting the new cloths do not forget about the necessity of broad-seaming them).

This inevitably makes both the foot and luff longer at

the same time. If it is required to make one longer without the other, it is necessary to enlarge both first, and then reduce one as described below.

The only other possible way of increasing the area is to add short lengths of cloth all the way up the leech, staggering the inner ends. This method has the same result as the first, but it is more difficult and less desirable, and we do not recommend it.

For vertical cut mainsails where the cloths lie parallel to the leech, additional cloths can easily be added to the leech, but again making both luff and foot longer together, a further reducing operation being again necessary if only one side is required to be lengthened.

Bermudian Mainsails (Reducing the area) (Fig. 30)

In order to maintain the angle between the cloths and leech at 90°, the leech can only be cut so that the new leech is parallel to it, though the other two sides can be cut in any way desired.

The cutting of the leech is simple, involving only the resetting of the headboard, the renewal of the head and clew patches and clew eyelet, and the refitting of the tabling. If the other two sides are cut, care should be taken that they are cut with the correct floor plan curves.

If it is desired to shorten either the luff or foot without the other there is only one correct way of doing it, this being to cut both the luff and foot, leaving the leech as it is (for shortening the foot, it is quite in order to cut the luff only if you do not mind the boom dropping). If, however, the reduction in area is only slight, it is very tempting to cut the leech regardless of the fact that the cloths will then no longer be at right angles, and in fact this can be done satisfactorily if the tabling is fitted more tightly than normal to compensate for the extra tendency in the cloth to stretch, being now cut slightly on the cross. As an indication as to whether it will be satisfactory to cut the leech in this way, we would say that the reduction in length should not exceed 10% of the whole length.

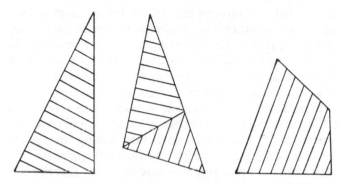

FIGS. 30–32. These plans are included to assist in deciding whether a proposed alteration is feasible. Copy the plan on a plain piece of paper and cut out. Then remove, insert or add pieces as necessary to produce a plan of the sail after alteration. Bearing in mind that the weave of the cloth must be parallel or at right angles to all unsupported sides, it will be clear whether or not the altered sail will be correctly cut.

Headsails (Enlarging) (Fig. 31)

In mitre-cut headsails, this is almost impossible, especially as an economic proposition. In vertical cut sails, additional cloths can be joined to the leech, ensuring that the new leech is parallel to the old, thus lengthening the foot and luff. In Scotch cut sails, where the cloths lie parallel to leech and foot, further cloths may be added to both leech and foot (but not to one of them) so that the new leech and foot are parallel to the old and the same distance from the old as each other.

Headsails (Reducing the Area) (Fig. 31)

The only practicable way to do this in mitre-cut sails is to cut off the luff wire and re-fit in any position that one likes. There are obvious limitations, but by diagrams it is easy to see whether it is possible to get the shape and size you want. It is merely unfortunate that by shortening the foot without the luff, the clew drops, but this is just one of the limitations. It is not possible to cut either the leech or foot, as these must remain at right angles to the cloths.

In addition to the above it is possible to shorten the luff by splitting the sail down the last seam, and taking out indentical 'V' pieces from each side, having their points the clew, closing the two halves of the sail where the 'V's' have been removed. It is of course necessary that the 'V's' should be the same in order that the seams each side should meet on the new last seam.

Gaff Mainsails (Enlarging) (Fig. 32)

Gaff mainsails are usually cut with the cloths parallel to the leech to give more strength to stand the strain between gaff and boom. So the only way of enlarging the sail is to fit extra cloths to the leech, so that the new leech is parallel to the old. This involves making both the head and foot longer. One of them could be reduced again by altering the other three sides, but almost certainly it would not be worth it.

Gaff Mainsails (Reducing area) (Fig. 32)

There is a certain amount of scope here, as the leech can be cut provided that the new leech is parallel to the old, and the other three sides may be cut in any way one pleases. It is just a question of studying the matter rather carefully in order to arrive at the sizes and shape one wants.

SAILMAKING IN TERYLENE

IN principle, the same rules apply to sailmaking in terylene as to the use of cotton. Terylene does, however, possess certain different properties, and is generally not quite so easily worked as cotton. The instructions throughout the book should be followed for terylene as for cotton, with the following differences:

Choice of Cloth

It is desirable to use the same, or nearly the same weight of terylene as for cotton. It is also a fact that the heavier the terylene the more easily will it sew without puckering. The material should be heat-set to reduce stretch on the bias to a minimum, and is best used in 18 in. or 36 in. cloths, as false seaming is not too satisfactory. The lesser stretch of the cloth makes narrower seams than 18 in. unnecessary.

All Floor Plans (with the exception of the spinnaker)

Terylene sails are cut full size and no stretching allowance is made. The maximum depth of round in each case is as follows:

Jib Luff: Nil from head to halfway between head and tack, then between the halfway point and the tack the round should be 1 in. in 12 ft. (12 ft. being the whole length of the luff).

Leech: as shown in diagram.

Foot: as shown in diagram. Extra area may be gained by a much larger round to the foot, the length of the foot tabling being shortened by means of darts from the foot tabling vertically into the sail, the resultant foot tabling being half an inch shorter in 6 ft. than the straight line behind between tack and clew.

Mainsail Luff: two-thirds that shown in diagram.

Foot and Leech: same as in diagram.

Note. The above depths of curve are for mainsails set on straight masts. For bending masts the luff should have the same curvature in addition to that of the mast when fully bent for close-hauled sailing.

Broad Seaming

This is not necessary in headsails. In Bermudian and Gunter mainsails, every seam should be broadened, curving to run into the ordinary seam at a soft line drawn from the head of the sail to a position one-third way along the foot from the tack; this line curving slightly in towards the luff if the head of the sail is required to be less full. The measurements given are for a luff of 20 ft.–25 ft. and should be scaled up for larger sails.

The tack seam should have an additional overlap of 1 in. (making 1½ in. in all) curving to nothing at the soft line. The width of extra overlap should be progressively less for each seam as the head of the sail is approached and should be proportional to the length of the luff. Thus the extra overlap is 1 in. at the tack, ½ in. half-way up, and a ¼ in. three-quarters of the way up. The same occurs for the foot seams, the extra overlap reducing to nothing at the soft line.

Gaff mainsails should be broadseamed in the same way as for cotton and flax.

An electric Terylene cutter (this can be made by grinding an electric soldering iron into a blade) can be used to cut away the surplus cloth in each broad seam; or the surplus cloth can be left in position. The cutter has the effect of sealing the edges of the cloth where it cuts, and is a very useful instrument throughout Terylene sailmaking, raw edges no longer needing to be turned in.

Machining (page 17)

Heat stretched terylene thread should be used, as it is imperative to use a thread which stretches as little as possible. The tensions on the machine should be adjusted very carefully with almost no pressure.

The two halves of the strike-up marks (page 47) should be matched very carefully, as it is more difficult in Terylene to smooth away puckers resulting from not quite matching them. An excellent method both to match the strike-up marks, and to make sure that the seam is not puckered in the stitching is to join the seam first by double-sided adhesive tape, sewing the seam through cloth and tape. It is desirable to ensure that the stitching is not too tight as puckers in seams sewn with synthetic threads will not come out in use as readily as those sewn in other types of thread.

Finishing

Terylene sails are ordinarily finished in exactly the same ways as for cotton, except: (*a*) the luff and foot ropes (Terylene) are fitted exactly the same length as the sail — they will shorten a little in the roping, allowing for slight stretch in setting to the marks; (*b*) foresail luffs must be fitted with plastic covered wire, whether this is galvanised or stainless, as either will react with Terylene if allowed contact with it. Nylon or stainless thimbles should be used, not galvanised ones.

The ends of Terylene rope can be sealed by melting obviating need for whippings when splicing, etc.

Terylene tape, either cut with a heat knife from the main cloth, or woven specially, can if desired be used instead of the ordinary type of tablings.

Luff and foot ropes, preferably braided may be fitted inside the tabling, rather than roped to the outside, if desired. The rope should be secured in the tabling either by a straight-stitch machine using a half-foot, or by hand, using a sticking stitch as for the luffs of headsails.

Note. No initial stretching is required for Terylene sails. If they do not set to begin with, they will not do so without alteration. Care should be taken to set mainsails exactly to their marks.

GLOSSARY

Aerofoil
> The wing of an aircraft.

ADM
> Abbreviation for sailcloth woven to Admiralty specification.

American cotton
> Cotton grown in U.S.A., mainly the Southern States.

Aspect ratio
> The ratio of foot to luff. Where the luff is 30 ft. and the foot 15 ft., the aspect ratio would be 1 : 2. An average ratio is in the region of 1 : 2½. For greater efficiency, racing yachts tend to a high aspect ratio, i.e. the luff being longer in relation to the foot.

Batten
> A flexible blade, made usually of hickory or plastic, fitted at right angles to the leech to hold out the curve of the leech.

Batten pocket
> A pocket stitched at right angles to the leech of a Bermudian mainsail to take the batten.

Beam
> The width of a boat.

Beeswax
> Wax used on hand sewing thread to make it sew more easily

Bermudian mainsail
> Jib headed mainsail, having only three sides, luff, leech and foot.

Bisect
   Draw a line dividing an angle exactly in half.

Bolt rope
   Rope sewn to the edge of the sail, normally sewn on the
   port side to assist in distinguishing the particular part of
   the sail being handled.

Boom
   Spar to which the foot of a sail is attached.

Broad-seam
   A seam in a sail which is gradually broadened to counteract additional and localised strain, as in the tack of a mainsail.

Clew
   The aft lower corner of a sail to which the sheet is attached.

Clew-liner
   A long thin patch running from the clew up along the
   leech to a position above the top reef.

Concave
   A hollow curve i.e. if the edge of a sail is cut as a concave
   curve, the line of cut will curve in towards the centre of the
   sail.

Convex
   Curving outwards from the centre of the material. The
   opposite of concave.

Cringle
   A loop of rope fitted to the edge of a sail through sewn
   eyelets and carrying a thimble. Used where considerable
   strain is taken by the sail.

Cross, cutting on the
   Material is cut on the cross if the cutting line lies at an
   angle to warp and weft.

Cross stitch

A zig-zag stitch made by a special cross stitch machine. Normally each stitch is at right angles to the one following, but the angle may be varied. As a rule, one side of the row of stitching lies on the seam of the sail, and the other just off, but both sometimes lie on the seam.

Dacron

The American equivalent of terylene, a synthetic fibre first produced in England. Special properties are very small amount of stretch, great strength and resistance to rot.

Duck

A general term applied to ordinary cotton canvas.

Egyptian cotton

Cotton grown in Egypt, extensively used for good quality sails.

Eyelet

A brass eyelet in two parts. One part is placed through a hole in the canvas, clamped to the part on the other side of the cloth by a special punch and die. Each size of eyelet needs a different punch and die.

Eye-splice

A splice producing a loop at the end of wire or rope.

False-seam

A seam made in a cloth by doubling the cloth in the form of a 'Z' and sewing down. False-seams are required where otherwise the sailcloth would be to wide.

Fid

A wooden spike for opening out cringles, grommets, etc. Large fids have a flat base for standing on the floor.

Finishing

The last operation in sailmaking, covering roping, fitting luff wire, etc. and in completing the sail.

Flat-seaming

Hand stitching from the top side of the cloth. This stitch is used in sewing the seams of a sail where these are sewn by hand for added strength (sails these days are rarely handsewn owing to the much greater cost).

Flax

Sailcloth woven from flax yarns, recognisable by coarser weave, and grey-brown colour. Properties are durability, resistance to tearing and rot, and greater stretch.

Flow

The curvature or belly in sails, induced by attaching convex curved sides of a sail to straight spars.

Foot

The lowest side of a sail.

Foot-liner

An elongated patch running along the foot of a sail, either from the tack or the clew. A clew foot-liner is used in all foresails, but in mainsails foot-liners are usually confined to larger sails.

Foresail

The sail set immediately forward of the mainsail. In the normal way this is a headsail, and is usually a staysail, but in, for instance, a schooner, it is the normal mainsail type sail fitted to the foremast.

Gaff

Spar to which the head of a gaff mainsail is fitted.

Gaff mainsail

A four-sided mainsail, the head fitted to a gaff.

Genoa

A long footed headsail, normally overlapping the mainsail to a marked degree.

Grommet

A ring of rope or wire formed by laying up a single strand, the strand completing the circle as many times as there were strands in the original from which the one strand was removed.

Groove, luff or foot

A groove in the mast or boom designed to hold the bolt rope of a sail. The slot is much narrower than the internal width of the groove, and in each case the bolt rope is fed into the groove at a position near the tack. The head and clew of the sail designed to fit grooved spars are made specially to fit.

Hand thread

Thread used in hand sewing, normally linen thread.

Hanks

Slides attached to luff or foot of sail designed to run in track fitted to mast or boom. The slides may be seized or shackled (with special shackles) to the sail. In the latter case care should be taken that the bolt rope is reinforced in way of each shackle to counteract chafe.

Head

The topmost side of a sail.

Headboard

An aluminium or wooden plate fitted in the peak of a Bermudian mainsail to gain sail area and to make the line of the leech, if produced, meet the top of the mast for better appearance.

Headsail

A general term covering jibs, staysails, jib topsails, yankees, etc.

Italian hemp

A high quality rope used extensively in the manufacture of cotton and flax sails, partly for its lasting qualities, but mainly as it stretches less than other ropes. It is usually lightly tarred for sailmaking.

K

Jib
>The foremost headsail, the clew being as a rule cut higher than in other headsails.

Jib topsail
>A jib set flying, usually having the peak at the mast-head.

Jute
>A fibre used, amongst other things, for making inferior quality canvas. It is sometimes mixed with flax.

Last seam
>The centre seam in a mitre-cut sail.

Leech
>The aft side of a sail.

Leech-line
>A thin line attached near the peak of a sail, running down the leech inside the tabling, emerging just above the clew. The line is tautened if there is a tendency for the leech to flap. The leech line is usually confined to Bermudian mainsails, but is sometimes fitted to Genoas.

Leeward
>The side facing the way the wind is blowing to.

Leeway
>Sideways drift of a hull to leeward.

Linear
>Measurements taken down the length. 10 linear yards would indicate that the cloth, whatever the width, was 10 yards long.

Linen
>A finer version of flax. Used in hand thread.

Liner
>An elongated patch running up the leech from the clew.

Long splice
>A splice to join the ends of rope, so made that the diameter of the rope at the join does not increase appreciably.

Loose-footed

Where the foot of the sail is not fitted to a spar. The clew of a loose-footed mainsail is sometimes fitted to a boom, the foot being left free.

Luff

The forward or leading edge of a sail.

Mainsail

A vessel's principal sail.

Marline

A strong tarred twine used for covering wire, splices etc. It is applied either by hand, with a serving mallet, the ball having to be passed round with each turn, or with a patent serving mallet having a bobbin attached.

Mildew-proofing

A chemical proofing applied in liquid form to a sail or to sailcloth. A sail can be dipped after manufacture, or the cloth can be proofed by the suppliers in the roll.

Mitre-cut

A cut where the cloths strike the leech and foot of a sail at right angles, meeting along a seam which bisects the clew.

Needle

The body of a sailmaker's needle is usually triangular, and can be obtained in varying sizes. Sewing machine needles also vary in size for different size threads.

Nylon

The first synthetic yarn used for sails. Its tendency to stretch precludes its use in all except spinnakers. Can rot in continuous sunlight.

Palm

A leather strap fitting the palm of the hand, having a hard serrated pad into which the eye of the sailmaker's needle fits, to enable the needle to be pushed from the centre of the palm.

K2

Parachute spinnaker

Equal sided spinnaker with considerable fulness, designed to set either way round and with either clew at the end of the spinnaker boom. The old fashioned type of spinnaker was narrower, triangular and with different length luff and foot.

Patches

Reinforcing cloth fitted at corners of sails and at specific points along the sides, e.g. at each end of a row of reef points.

Peak

The topmost corner of a sail.

Piping foot

A one-sided foot of a sewing machine designed to enable the machine to sew a row of stitches close up against the piping.

Piston hank

A spring loaded hank shaped to fit the luff wire of a head-sail and to clip the forestay.

Punch and die

Specially designed to clamp the two sides of brass eyelets together, or to clamp the brass ferrule into a sewn eyelet. A different set of punches and dies is required for each size eyelet and for each size sewn eyelet.

Reef

An arrangement for reducing temporarily the area of a sail. A reef is taken either by tying the sail down to the boom by means of a row of reef points placed parallel to the foot, or by rolling the boom round and winding the sail round it.

Roller reefing

Taking a reef by rolling the boom and winding the sail up round it.

Roping
Sewing a bolt rope to a sail.

Round-seaming
Hand-sewing two or more parts of cloth together by sewing across their edges, the resultant stitch running round and round along the edge of the cloth.

Rubbing down
Making the sail ready for roping and finishing after the cloths have been sewn together.

Sail hook
A metal hook with a sharp point attached by a thin line to a point on the right hand side of the seated hand-finisher, hooking into the sail which is being roped or finished, either through an eyelet or into the cloth, to enable the edge of the sail to be held out tight.

Scotch cut
A mitre-cut sail where the cloths lie parallel to leech and foot, meeting on the centre seam bisecting the clew.

Seam
The join between the cloths in a sail.

Selvedge
A non-fraying edge of a cloth produced in the weave. A straight selvedge is desirable in laying the cloths of a sail.

Serve
To cover a wire or splice by winding marline tightly round it.

Sewing guide
A line a short distance from the edge of the cloth to indicate the extent of the overlap between this cloth and the next.

Sewn eyelet
An eyelet in the sail formed by sewing a brass ring in position over the hole. The sewn eyelet is much stronger than the ordinary punched eyelet.

Sheet

A rope attached to the clew of a sail for adjusting the set.

Slide

A hank fitted to luff or foot or a sail designed to fit a track attached to mast or boom.

Spike

A metal sharp pointed tool used in wire splicing and for turning shackle pins.

Spinnaker

A lightweight voluminous sail designed especially for use in a following wind.

Splice

The joining of wire or rope by the intertwining of the strands in a predetermined way known to provide adequate strength.

Staysail

The headsail set immediately forward of the mainsail.

Sticking stitch

A stitch largely used close up to the luff wire of a headsail passing alternatively through and back along the tabling.

Straight stitch

The stitch sewn by a normal sewing machine.

Strainer

An elongated patch, similar to the clew liner, but fitted elsewhere — bisecting the clew or tack, along foot from clew or tack, down leech from peak, etc. The larger the sail the more strainers may be necessary.

Stretching allowance

The allowance made in drawing the full size sail plan on the floor for the cloth to stretch in use. Allowances vary for different cloths.

Strike-up marks

Short pencil lines placed at short intervals across the join of each cloth as laid on the floor plan. The two halves of each mark must be made to match when the cloths are sewn together to ensure that the cloths are sewn as laid.

Tabling

The doubling of the edge of a sail by the addition of an extra strip of cloth for strength. The weave of the tabling should lie in the same direction as in the sail beneath it.

Tack

The forward lower corner of a sail.

Tack angle

The angle the foot makes to the luff. In the average mainsail this is 87°.

Tail

The end of a rope which has been brought to a fine point.

Tapered splice

A splice joining two ends of rope of different sizes.

Terylene

A synthetic yarn used in sailcloth. Special properties are strength, lack of stretch, resistance to rot. (For details of sailmaking in terylene, see Appendix, p. 126.)

Thimble

A round or heart-shaped metal fitting designed to fit tightly in eye-splices, cringles, etc.

Throat

The corner of a sail between the head and the luff.

Topsail

The sail set above a gaff mainsail.

Turnover

A sewn eyelet fitted with brass ferrule.

Vertical cut

The cut of a sail where the cloths lie parallel to the leech

Warp

The yarns running lengthways in a piece of cloth.

Weft
> The yarns running across a piece of cloth.

Whipping
> The binding of a rope end by winding twine round it and securing. Its purpose is to stop the rope end fraying.

Windward
> Facing the direction from which the wind is blowing.

Wire luff
> The luff of a sail in which a wire is incorporated.

Wire-to-rope splice
> A splice joining one end of rope to one end of wire.

Yankee
> A large stem-to-masthead foresail, having large area and usually being in lightweight cloth.

Zig-zag stitch
> The stitch made by a cross-stitch machine for sewing the seams of sails.

INDEX